Finding Y(Mom's Guide to the Universe

MW00964911

Jen Brunett

JEN BRUNETT

Copyright © 2014 Jen Brunett

All rights reserved.

ISBN-10: 0692292667
ISBN-13: 978-0692292662 (Triple Moon)

DEDICATION

I dedicate this book to my mother, Joyce Grabowski. I pray that you have your own guidebook up there in heaven and will read it to me when it's time to sing "Tiny Dancer" again. I love you!

CONTENTS

JEN BRUNETT

ACKNOWLEDGMENTS

I'd like to acknowledge my two incredible little miracles, Cash and Jagger. While I jest, sharing the crazy stories I have to tell about the two of you, please know that you have taught me more about myself and the world around us than any one ever could. Without you, this book would not be here. I will love you to infinity and beyond.

To my husband, Tommy. Thanks for kicking me in the rear and telling me to write a book already. You are the most gifted and captivating person I have ever had the pleasure to meet and the fact that we are partners for life is surreal. I am one lucky Polish lady! Together, the four of us can heal the world through music, creativity, the written word, and laughter. I love you.

To my father, Dennis. Dad, I know what I went through when mom passed but I cannot imagine the pain that you had to endure during that terrible time. From you I have inherited my unusual sense of humor and ability to make light of the most bleak of situations. I'm proud that you are my father, thank you for raising me to be the person I am today.

To Tre of Tre Gallery for lending me your creativity and designing my beautiful book cover art and photos!

To my mentor, Pastor Robin. The day I walked in your door I knew that I had found a safe place to share, grow, and learn with love, light, and most importantly, humor. Thank you for your wisdom, grace, and belief in me—in all of us.

To my mentor, Dr Frances Carns. It feels like ages ago when I used to sit in that little room in the attic. I cannot tell you the impact that those days have had on my life and I carry the wisdom with me to this day. Thank you for shining your incredible light on those who need it.

To my mentor and soul mommy, Cindy Lee. Thank you for imparting your wisdom onto me and all of your students.

To my very own Jiminy Cricket, Joanie Strulowitz. Thank you for your honest opinions, constant encouragement, and wisdom as a writer and friend.

To family and friends. You know who you are and I love you.

INTRO

If you are anything like me, then you are probably sitting on the toilet reading this, holding the door shut with one hand while saying (politely or otherwise) "Just a minute, honey, Mommy's almost done."

If not on the toilet then perhaps you are standing up somewhere in another part of the house within earshot of the kids not daring to sit down because the book will immediately fly from your hands as kids have a special radar for mommy at rest—or possibly you're walking around with a little monkey clinging to your leg. However it is that you find that moment of you-time, I want to thank you for spending it with me.

Okay, let's get down to business. Have you ever seen that cartoon television show with the little baby that has a head shaped like a football? You know the one… there's a big man with half a brain posing as a father, with a chin that is shaped like something that probably shouldn't be on prime time? You SO know what and who I'm talking about, don't you?

There's an episode where the baby walks up to his mom all innocent and says this for five minutes straight, "Mom! Mommy! Mom! Mom! Mommy! Ma, Ma, Ma! MOM!"

In the mean time the mom is laying in bed staring straight ahead at the wall in front of her with a look in her eyes that says "I am soooo drained and need to acknowledge you but what could you possibly want at this moment right now after I've taken care of every one of your needs five seconds ago?!"

Finally, her breaking point is reached and the disgruntled mom shouts an extremely irritated, "WHAT?!" to her son, in which the two year old football head baby replies, "Hi!" with an accomplished smile, a snide giggle and trots away.

I LOVE being a mom and feel blessed that I have been able to create life, give birth, and nourish these little miracles but every so often (using that term loosely) I get my own football head kind of day.

     I must admit that I had sort of a hard adjustment to motherhood in the beginning as many of us surprisingly do. I suffered postpartum depression with both of my boys. I was living in downtown New York City on the 31st floor with my husband and absolutely no family around. None of our friends had children and I had no experience with kids. Really, I mean NONE. I can count on one hand the number of times I babysat in my entire life. While I was excited to start this new adventure with a family of my very own, I was also a little scared of all the unknowns of parenting.

     Like, why didn't a personalized manual just pop out after the placenta, catered to my baby's individual needs?

     The reality hit when I brought my newborn baby boy home in the summer of 2007. He was three weeks early, very tiny and he slept A LOT during the day. When he was sent home, the doctor said he was a little jaundice and to contact them if he was too sleepy.

     Well what does that mean? Aren't newborns supposed to be sleepy??

     When he was two days old and after a very long stretch of sleeping the entire afternoon, I figured I should try and wake him up to feed him. Well… he wouldn't wake up. He was breathing fine but I absolutely could not wake him up! I stared at him and poked him like the internet told me I should—to check for the "yellow" color of jaundice. I compared the (gentle) poke marks to lemons, computer paper, LEMONADE!

     What color yellow is too yellow?!

     Now that I was in a full blown panic I called the doctor, and he said to take the baby back to the hospital for a check-up. I was terrified and so positive there HAD to be something wrong and immediately rushed out the door to (literally) run him to the hospital.

     I did say we were in Manhattan, right? Everything is in within walking distance there. I was also a brand new city mom and realized quickly the reason why I saw those strollers with monster truck wheels all over the place, especially downtown. My little travel system with the barbie car sized wheels wasn't cutting the cheese when it came to the obstacle course-like street terrain! Needless to say, WHILE I was running I had to push the stroller with one hand and hold on to the baby's head with the other to keep him still and comfortable. Along the way, I nearly plowed over Tyra Banks' paparazzi! If it weren't for me screaming, "Get out of my way!" to the herd of photogs then they would have been tossing lenses for sure!

Ah, New York moments. Thankfully he was fine and totally woke up when the doctor finally came to see him. With one incident down, it was time for my next hurdle.

Night time with my son was a little rough but I was able to do all of those things new moms were supposed to like sleep when the baby slept, watch the myriad of little adorable faces he made as he drifted off to dreamland, and clean up projectile poop from the wall six feet away in the middle of the night. (No lie, I have witnesses as my husband was the one who was changing him at the time!)

We fell into a mini newborn baby routine until he hit two weeks old. This is when my ideals of all those perfect, quiet, sleeping, playful babies I've seen my whole life on shows and movies went out like a night light on my sleep deprived semi-hallucinating brain. (I will not even speak of the floating blonde haired baby I saw one time at three in the morning, circling ABOVE my son's co sleeper.) but I got used to the sleeplessness. I didn't complain (much) because I had somehow managed to work it out between the two of us.

I had always heard that once you get settled into a routine with a baby it would change instantaneously. Honestly, I never really knew what that meant and merely smiled and nodded when I heard the advice. When my little guy turned two weeks old though, the advice light bulb didn't just go off above my clueless head, it blew and shattered and I was left blindly trying to pick up the pieces stepping on diaper fragments and pacifiers along the way.

Suddenly my sleepy adorable little cherub who loved to play (think stare at the ceiling) in his little wicker baby moses basket was no longer content in his hip blue surroundings. Oh no… he was ready to move out of his minuscule studio apartment on the coffee table and take habit somewhere that allowed him to live the vertical life. He decided then and there he would not leave his mother's arms, ever! And she must not sit. She must constantly be in motion. If she did not move, he would scream as though the stillness pained him to the very core.

If he did happen to take a nap, which would usually happen in his car seat as we walked endlessly around Tribeca (this time sporting a more appropriate stroller with monster truck wheels) no matter where we were, at exactly 7pm, he would wake up frantic, screaming in terror. This would continue hour upon hour and absolutely NOTHING would solace the cries. Of course the doctors wouldn't listen to me when I told them that my baby was sick, had an allergy, reflux, or SOMETHING! They said he was fine but I felt otherwise.

Babies are not supposed to cry this much, right? They sleep sometimes don't they? Mine sure didn't!

Turns out my baby boy had what the doctors like to call, "colic." My own personal definition of colic (besides living hell) stands as,

"Your son is in a whole mess of stomach pain but we can't do anything about it so deal with it until he turns 12 weeks old or more in some cases."

The next few weeks made life nothing short of miserable but the good news was that I lost most of my baby weight circling our little apartment for hours every night. He'd usually pass out around midnight with me shortly thereafter followed by the nightly ritual of waking every thirty minutes. We were pretty pooped by sunrise.

From the enlightened words of John Lennon, "Life is what happens to you while you're busy making other plans," and that is exactly what happened to us. The baby grew out of his colic, we got his sleep under control, and he turned into an excellent napper and night sleeper by seven months. The next three months were smooth sailing until we hit an unexpected sand bar.

It was early spring and I had made a desperate phone call to my friend. As soon as I heard her familiar voice I immediately began cursing obscenities and I'm pretty sure speaking in strange foreign tongues. She listened to my otherworldly fits for a few minutes and seized the moment when I took a long deep breath as an opportunity to ask me a question before I began ranting again.

"Are you pregnant?"

I stopped my rage, succumbed to the inevitable and voiced a resounding, "Yes. Yes I Am."

While the energy of pure joy did eventually settle in, those telltale pink lines on the little stick I was holding in my hand emitted from my small frame a primal fear that I had already blocked from my mind.

"Please, oh please do not let the colic take over my new baby!"

As luck had it, it didn't. My second son was born nine months later without a hitch. He didn't even cry; my almost ten pounder just scanned the hospital room with wide eyes and stuck his tongue out, tasting the air like a lizard. Except he wasn't a reptile. As my creative husband suggested, he more resembled that of a chubby businessman getting ready to dust himself off and hit the bus for work. He was just missing a cigar, briefcase, and at least 30 years of life on earth.

Cute as a button and stubborn as his mama, we were officially four and I was in the trench's of horrible depression. At one point baby number one was screaming because he wanted attention, baby number two was screaming because he was hungry, hated formula and breast milk (he still refuses milk most of the time to this day) and I was sitting on the living room floor crying because I didn't know how to handle the screaming babies.

I felt as though I was the epitome of "Epic Fail Mommy" and had sunk to new levels of rock bottom. This is when the chapter ended and we moved Upstate. Just like that. Within weeks we were out of the city and closer to family and old friends. While I still felt like a failure I think the huge life change did all of us some good.

Back in Manhattan, our apartment became entirely too small for the four of us. We had a quaint concrete balcony that we covered with astro turf to mimic a yard for the boys, complete with a tiny inflatable baby pool for the hot summer months. My husband and my older son were sharing a bedroom, the new baby had ours and I took up real estate on the living room couch as I was trying to figure out a way to get him to sleep through the night. By the way, that didn't come for quite a few years later!

Now in Upstate, we had our own house with bedrooms enough for all of us, a gas fireplace and a small yard with a fence and real live grass…and bees and bugs… but real grass just the same.

To my chagrin, I again found myself depressed. This time it was a longing for my beloved New York City and the friends we made there who were and always will be, like family. I missed the school I was going to before my first son was born, when I was well on my way to completing my Master's degree in Chinese Medicine and starting my career in the holistic health field. Instead I was a stay-at-home mom in a place that should be so familiar to me but instead left me feeling foreign and alone. I felt that there was something missing from my life, something that I couldn't put my finger on. I suppose I was at a point where I believed that I just couldn't win no matter which way I turned… but then something happened. A small spark ignited inside of me and I just couldn't ignore it.

A little over ten years prior to all of this, I began my studies with reading tarot cards intuitively as well as developing skills in mediumship. In 2001 I had completed my Reiki Master (a form of holistic healing) training which happened to be the same year that my mother had passed away from a brief illness. I know now it was her passing that made me push away my spiritual studies. I was mad, mad,

mad at whomever took her away too young and discovered the horrible irony that my strong foundation in spirituality could be ignored as I watched her suffer and die as I held her hand.

Ironically, it was she who lit the spiritual match AFTER her passing. I explain in detail later on but it all has to do with a dream I had and the important message she had for me!

Previous to that I had attended meditation classes regularly, took other workshops of varying metaphysical topics, and studied with people of like-mind. Even though I had practiced Reiki and tarot at home in Upstate as well as Manhattan, I realized that I had let that spiritual side of me slip away as I was caught up in the grueling hours of studying for my degree and the enticing bright lights that night time in the city dazzled me with.

I soon discovered that the spark that heated me up as I was feeling emotionally chilly was the other side of my life, the spiritual side, that I had nearly forgotten about but was now beckoning me to pay attention.

Pay attention, I did. During our first summer back home, my husband and I were discussing the prospects of me starting my own business of doing Reiki and readings on a professional level and spirit answered in the best way possible.

The very next day after the decision was made, someone called and offered me a Reiki table for nothing more than a reading and a hug. One week later, a place to practice just dropped into my lap. I didn't even have to look for it, it found me! This literally happened without announcing to ANYONE of my intentions of starting a business. It was just simple in-passing conversation about what it is that I do. Suddenly phone reading clients were coming in from around the country and I was sharing the Reiki love with many!

Around that time too, I started writing again. Next to music and spirituality, writing is one of my biggest passions in life. I made my own business website, started a blog based on the stuff I love, and began dreaming up and submitting articles in virtual and paper publications. I also began writing my own guided meditations and leading classes which, to my surprise, people actually seemed to like attending!

Then it just all sort of fell into place. While I had thought I had lost my sense of spirituality, I really had it all along. I had forgotten to use that side of my life as a guide to get me through all of the tough as well as easy times I'd experienced in the previous seven(ish) years.

I began developing my own heart lead and intuitive guided practice of living more with love and spirituality every day and honestly have never looked back. Times still get tough as we can all expect and I still suffer with anxiety yet I find the meaning of every single day to be deeper than I had ever imagined.

Back when the babies were born if I had been more in-tune with myself than I would have breezed through some of those early days. Well maybe not breezed… but I could have sorted through a deeper understanding of what early motherhood was meant to be. I would have meditated during the middle of the night when I was awake breastfeeding in bed instead of crying and watching music videos on VH1. I would have breathed more and worried less, I would have spoken with the babies' angels and help them set baby intentions.

Shoulda, coulda, woulda… right?

My story is the foundation for the intention of this book. I wanted to give other moms just like me a chance to explore their spiritual side. I want women (and men because dads raise babies too!) to know that it is perfectly okay and super important to develop a sense of self-love by exploring all that is deeply meaningful to you while you are simultaneously handling the most important job of your life, raising mini reflections of yourself. Our children do mirror our expressions, attitudes, actions, and reactions. If we come from a place of love and worth then they will too!

My wish for you is to explore all of the wonderful things that reside deep inside of you—to reflect your children's curiosities as though you're also seeing everything for the first time, and live life with love and hopeless abandon. May these pages act as a match to help ignite the spiritual spark inside of you.

A GUIDE FOR THE GUIDE

There are a couple of different ways that you can use this book.

You can read through it like any old book for entertainment and hopefully come away with a couple of memorable nuggets that stick with you for whatever reason. You can also check the table of contents and skip around to the various pieces that strike your fancy, then use the rest for fire kindling. (Unless it's electronic. Then just delete it.)

OR

You can get yourself a journal, notepad, a marker and some toilet paper, or whatever happens to be convenient at the moment and work with this book in your own time, on your own terms. TRY the various exercises that I've carved out for people such as myself with a next to nothing time span for self indulgence or personal attention. Relax and know there's no time limit for getting through this book. If you try out ONE single thing from any chapter and have either liked it or hated it then you have succeeded.

Succeeded in what? You have started the process of freeing your mind and becoming open to the possibility of gaining balance by honoring your spiritual self.

What will it be then? The red pill or the blue? Ok, ok I just HAD to throw in a random movie reference from *The Matrix*. I'm soooo not talking narcotics—it's my geeky way of asking which choice will you make? Work with it or read it and leave it alone. It's all up to you!

CRESCENDO

Close your eyes just for a moment and think of your favorite song. When you figure out what that is, how about playing it one time through? Put the book down, find the song, close your eyes, and listen. Take note of where the music leads you. Feel how it touches you from the inside out.

Isn't it amazing how music can appear to transcend any mood, lift your heart and touch your soul like nothing else can? It truly seems to trigger an other-worldly emotion where just for a couple of minutes, nothing else matters but you and the song.

Likewise, think of the moment when your child was born or when you met your child for the first time. Put yourself in that space where for an instant, the pain is gone, time stands still, and you are swirling in a state of total euphoria. There is no way to describe that feeling, is there? It seems to exist half on this plane and half in some other realm where nothing else matters except for you and your new baby. It is at that moment when everything in your world is absolutely perfect.

That feeling, that experience of bliss is similar to when you first discover the spiritual person that is harbored inside of yourself. Discovering your soul path is like waking up from a deep sleep and experiencing the world for the first time in a different light with new eyes. Living your path is what helps you to maintain much needed balance throughout your day. Spirituality helps you to grow as a being living on this physical plane and to cope with daily stresses in a more balanced and relaxed manner. It keeps you grounded and centered, yet always growing intellectually and comes with the understanding that we are all connected in some way.

Maintaining a spiritual equilibrium allows you to see your place in this world, feel your part in it, and keeps you afloat during those not so balanced moments when you want to purchase a one-way ticket to Siberia.

Being spiritual doesn't mean that you have to give up your current faith or religion. If anything, it serves to help you gain a better relationship with your own understanding of the divine. As you continue to discover more about who you are as a spiritual person the deeper your connection to your faith will be.

The feeling, the energy you experience when you hear your favorite song, witness the birth of your new baby, or set your eyes on a beautiful sunset has its own way of hitting that ethereal chord that connects you to some hidden place as though the chord is made of pure love and you are attached securely to the great unknown.

Throughout these pages you'll find different tools, tricks, lessons and guidance to finding your own spirit so that your personal understanding of the "great unknown" will become a known, true friend and companion to help you on your life's journey.

ENERGY AND CONNECTEDNESS

Since you are a parent (or going to be) you come pre-equipped with a fundamental knowledge base in regards to the science behind that six-letter word, known as "Energy." If you don't know what I'm talking about, go ahead and give your child (niece, nephew, kid down the street) a chocolate bar and a full glass of soda. That, my friend, will result in a massive display of energy expenditure!

We know energy as the force behind all living beings. It's that intangible "thing" that keeps the kids going like energizer bunnies, it's the heat we feel on our faces at the beach and what motivates a flower to bloom in spring. We create energy, are made up of energy and it exists all around us.

When dealing with "universal" and/or "spiritual" energy you'll find that not only is it a force that motivates and propels living beings into action but it is also very tangible. It is easier than you think to grasp this energy and harness it to bring balance and positive changes into your life as well as to aid in the lives of those you love.

For thousands of years, the Chinese believed that we have a system of energy running through our bodies that looks much like a road map containing our vital life force or "Qi." When our Qi is blocked, we become ill. If the energy is moving freely then we feel well and complete. The Yogis believe their "life force energy" is called, Prana. The Japanese call this same energy, Ki. It is this energy that you balance when you meditate, do yoga, receive a healing, eat well, sleep well, and pretty much maintain a "balanced" lifestyle.

Did you roll your eyes after reading that last sentence? I sure did! How is it even possible to maintain balance with kids, partners, jobs, friends, family, LIFE?! It is difficult but not impossible.

Remember that thoughts are THINGS and you put positive energy in motion by creating a positive thought. Speaking that thought propels the energy forward like the contents of your baby's tummy ALWAYS does as soon as you put on a clean shirt. Ok that's gross I know, but isn't it so true?!

As I was saying: Thinking creates energy, speaking your thoughts out loud propels those thoughts into action. The same goes for negative energy! Send it out there and what will happen? It will come right back to you!

Let's get that energy going by speaking this out loud:

"I have the power within me to balance my life and live in harmony with my surroundings."

Think it, say it, mean it. Your life will transform as you transform your thinking. Try the above mantra or come up with something that resonates with you. Just keep it positive, people!

There is another thing about energy that amazes me. It isn't just some untouchable force that only a Jedi Knight can master (oh my glob, I have to stop with my geek references) it connects us to each other, to ourselves, and to our understanding of the divine.

Here's a cool story to prove my point. Ever since I was a little girl, I've always felt "connected" to something that I could not see. I didn't grow up particularly religious saving most of my church experiences for weddings, funerals, easter basket blessings (as many Polish people do) and the occasional game of Bingo. I sort of understood the religious figures placed high above us on the walls of the church and always adored the ones of Mary holding the little baby, but I never truly knew their stories or developed a close personal connection to them until many years later.

No, this was a different "something" that I was connected to. I always felt drawn to it, talked to it (I was even busted having a full on conversation in mid air with it by my mother and brother once. Yikes.) prayed to it, cried to it, you name it. I suppose now when I look back, that "something" would now be considered god/goddess/the divine/the universe or whatever your understanding is. I think I knew that then but didn't really consider it. It wasn't until I took courses in energy healing that I finally understood what that connection was.

My first experience was profound and what I gathered from it, has stuck with me as a basis towards my personal belief system ever since. I was 21 years old, and on this particular day I had just experienced close to six hours worth of first degree Reiki training. Reiki (pronounced ray-key) is a Japanese form of hands on healing in which you go through a series of initiations that allow you to be connected to the Reiki energy and utilize it to heal yourself and others. It sounds bizarre but it really works in ways I can't even begin to explain and am certainly not scientific enough to try!

At this point in the class I had already experienced meditation, history, hand positions, and now it was time for the big initiation. I was SO excited because Reiki had always felt so magical to me and still does, honestly, because it certainly carries an air of mystery. It's a mystery because we don't know how it works and I'm hoping that in this lifetime our brilliant scientists will find the answer. Until then, we have to hold onto faith that it works in some unknown way. At least now I know how the early settlers felt when they thought the world was flat!

At the pivotal moment of my Reiki initiation, my eyes were closed, my hands were held in prayer position by my chest and I sat in silence waiting for my instructor to do whatever things she does to ease my body into the "system." I could feel her walking around me, doing something with her hands, and then she put them lightly on my head as if I was receiving a healing from her. I could feel the familiar comfy warmth that only Reiki energy can give but then something else happened as well. An extremely clear vision popped out of nowhere, which surprised me because I am not a hugely visual person. I saw what can only be described as a spiderweb. Except this web must have been home to Paul Bunyan's house spider because it was the biggest web I had ever seen—I imagined that it must have spanned the entire universe because I couldn't find its edges, there was no beginning or end; it simply went on and on. Upon closer inspection I noticed that on every little fiber of the web rested what appeared to be minuscule versions of every living thing on the planet! There were people and trees, animals, bugs…everything! After a moment however, the amazement turned into bewilderment as I noticed there was a blank spot on the spiderweb. A void where no living thing seemed to take up residence and when I tried to focus on it, the entire web completely vanished.

The fact that it disappeared seriously bummed me out because I knew I had just witnessed something really special, profound even, and was hoping that I would be able to catch it again. This is when it got even cooler. I thought the vision was simply gone until I decided to take a closer look around my meditative environment. Little did I know that I was in for a breathtaking surprise. All around me was this translucent web, glistening like raindrops in the sun. I could FEEL everything around me. It was like I was connected to everything on this web and everything was connected to me. To say I was shocked and humbled was an understatement. I was in awe and simply allowed myself to bask in the energy and the knowledge that I was but a tiny piece of the greater whole yet still an integral part of the entire equation. I just sat in this space blissfully until my initiation was over, all in a span of under ten minutes.

I really believe that I had uncovered something extraordinary, an answer that I've been searching for my entire young life. This, I believe, is one of the reasons why we can feel an argument that has just taken place when we walk into a room, even though we didn't witness the argument ourselves. It's the reason we have a sense about a person's friendliness without knowing anything about them or can pick up the phone to call someone we haven't spoken with in ages and suddenly see their number on the caller ID as they are dialing us at that exact moment. It's because of our connection to each other through this "web" that I saw during my initiation.

As someone who's been doing intuitive readings for many years, I've learned that this "spider web" could indeed be symbolic of some sort of energy field that we have yet to understand. It could be quantum physics, it could even be woo woo nonsense but it was real enough for me to actually believe that it is there in whatever form.

As I've grown, I realized that it's possible that we are all connected to some sort of ethereal web that we cannot see but can feel—kind of like a series of invisible phone lines that keep us plugged in or tuned into each other in subtle yet palpable ways. I also believe that this "web" is a way to explain our sixth sense, and maybe even another realm that's not far from our understanding of what may lie on the "other side." I've always been told that God is everywhere all around us... maybe that visual was another divine creation to help me put to all into perspective.

Whatever it is, it certainly explains a lot! It explains how we are all just a tiny piece of this fantastic puzzle and it takes a lot of small pieces to make the whole complete. Attitudes like bitterness, anger, hurt, resentment, jealousy, all resonate through the web and can be felt by every living being. Likewise, if you fill your heart with thoughts of love, peace, kindness, and joy not only to others but to YOURSELF as well, those on every part of the web will receive these impressions. Which emotion would you like to have gravitate towards you at any given time? I choose love, personally.

Understanding our connection to the greater whole is one more step towards becoming more in-tune and balanced spiritually. The key is not to believe in my crazy web meditation experience unless you would like to explore that idea further. You have to find and witness your own truths in a way that feels right to you and you'll know you've found it because the muscles in your heart will smile!

Finding your own personal connection is an excellent catalyst for spiritual growth. Once you recognize it, perhaps the next time you are alone in nature, playing with your children, sitting in a church pew or wherever you find spiritual support, you will notice an even greater sense of closeness and awareness to your understanding of the divine than you had before. Let's see if we can start making that connection!

SPIRIT SPEAK

When you open the doors to your spirituality, you are essentially walking into a whole new universe of possibilities. This new universe thrives on love, acceptance, and has its own unique language. Yes, language!

When we pray, dream, meditate, talk to ourselves, wish and hope, we send open ended questions out to the universe—to God, our angels, and the divine. Usually when we do this we desperately need answers but most often believe that from somewhere deep within, these answers will never come. Usually when we send out these often pleading questions, it's more of an expression for us, a way to communicate our troubles and let them go hoping something from beyond will hear us and answer. Some people just know with all of their heart they have been heard and others can only wish that they have.

I'm here to tell you that you've always been given answers even though you may not realize it! This is one of those times where I believe an example would be the best explanation, otherwise you may as well think that I've gone off the deep end.

When I was 23 years old, my mother died from lung cancer. It was a few short months between diagnosis to death and needless to say it changed our lives. My family has never been the same but we managed to move forward.

Mom used to carry cherry-menthol flavored cough drops with her for as long as I remember because of her persistent cough. That crinkly red bag was always peaking out of a corner in her purse; a heap of white wrappers taking residence on the nightstand next to her bed. I haven't tried one since she left but I can still remember the eucalyptus mixed with that maraschino cherry like flavor that lingers and makes food taste awful—kind of like drinking milk after brushing your teeth. Ew.

I lost faith in a lot of things after she passed as I've mentioned before. Of course, being involved in the type of work that I do (intuitive readings, energy healing) I totally expected to have some sort of sign from her. I asked the stars. I pleaded with heaven. I visited a psychic or two and still nothing. I really started to abandon my beliefs at this point, thinking that I must be crazy to even consider that this type of work can be real. I mean, I lost my mom way too early and I've heard NOTHING from her even though we had a discussion before she passed that she should try and get a hold of me from the other side. Well it was more me who had the discussion with her.

Her answer was, "Your grandmother and her friend tried that once."

"Well what happened?" I asked.

"Nothing."

That was all she said and I never talked about it with her again, even though I wanted to! I wanted to make some sort of plan for her to contact me in the afterlife but how could I dare press that sort of issue? It wasn't about me trying to prove in the existence of life after death. I was beside myself in anguish that she was going to die, and I couldn't do anything about it. I wanted to be selfish and find a way for her to stay with me always.

Instead, I let her go.

She decided to refuse chemotherapy after one round as it was only a means to keep her comfortable and not extend the life that she had left. After she passed, I tried to keep my faith even though my heart had shrunken. I continued to bide my time with studying holistic medicine figuring that there had to be a way to help other people that were in the same boat she was in. There had to be some sort of remedy to help people while they were fighting for their lives, and take care of the families whose loved one's fate became completely out of their control. Reiki was the only tool in my belt but instead of utilizing it for the greater good, I left it behind and took a personal hiatus from it, from meditation, from everything.

I don't remember when I stopped looking to the sky for answers but eventually I became more focused on what was right in front of me instead of up and/or within. In my heart though, was always that intense longing to hear from my mother.

One night, to my utter surprise, it happened.

I had gone to bed quietly without asking for signs or saying good night and I know I fell asleep rather quickly. I then had a dream that I was walking in an attic with two rooms in it. Mom and I were standing in one room and she kept motioning for me (she never talks in my dreams) to go in the other room but I was a little weary because it was snowing in there. Yes, snowing. But Mom said I had to go so, reluctantly, I did as I was told.

It wasn't cold. Of course it wasn't, I was dreaming! The room was entirely empty save for an old, weather-worn wooden table directly in the middle of it. As I approached this table I realized that placed on top was an empty bag of Mom's signature cough drops. I picked it up and immediately looked to the other room where I thought she was standing. She wasn't there anymore, which didn't bother me at all in my dream state, so I looked down at the bag with a smile remembering her. I'm not sure what it was but I suddenly felt the need to take a closer look, to inspect the words on the bag. I held it close to my line of vision so I could read the fine print under the block letter title of the cough drops. Do you know what was written there?

For Better Hearing Only

I woke up right at that point and immediately started laughing. Mom, apparently, had been trying to give me signs all along and obviously I wasn't listening! She had to force me into the snowy attic to give me the communication I'd been waiting for. I've had other good signs since but nothing so profound as that one!

The moral of the story here is this. Loved ones who have crossed over may not be able to communicate with you in the traditional sense. They may not be able to slam a door when you ask or turn on a light but they come to you in subtle ways. It could be a fleeting thought that wasn't your own, a song on the radio, a name overheard in a restaurant conversation or just an overwhelming feeling in your heart. So please keep talking to them and know they are still here with you listening, watching, and helping—or you may get reprimanded just as I did for being so stubborn!

I use the example for loved ones crossing over as I pick up on these energies quite often with my work with intuitive tarot, mediumship and Reiki. Symbolism in the spirit world is not just limited to psychic work though, it happens to us all, it's just a matter of opening our eyes, ears, and hearts to listen to it.

To really sum up what I'm trying to say here, when you say a prayer, talk to your guides, read your cards, or do whatever you like to do to communicate with your spiritual self you may think it is a one sided conversation but it rarely is. You have to be aware of the signs and symbolism all around you. You may hear a song being repeated over and over to which you can go to the lyrics, title, or even the artist to figure out what message could be waiting for you. The same name may continuously come up in conversation or even be overheard as you pass by people talking on the street. Colors may become more obvious, certain animals may appear to you suddenly. Spirit communication has endless possibilities.

It helps to pay attention to everything around you to "hear" the answers. Don't always just chalk things up to coincidence. You may have missed your message that way!

I wish I could tell you why you can't just get a knock on your door from a spiritual postal worker handing you a letter telling you all that you need to know. I suppose if I had to theorize it, we aren't given all the answers because if it were that easy, we would have nothing to learn. Life is a series of personal choices and decisions and what you receive from your deeper intuitive self, from your guides or angels, are merely suggestions. "[They] can only show you the door, you're the one who has to walk through it." (Oh wow, another *Matrix* quote...Princess Geekness at your service!)

***

I bet this all sounds overwhelming, doesn't it? You're probably like, "Okay pay attention to my surroundings. Check! Anything could be symbolic of an answer. Check, check."

Then you look around to sort of scan your environment and think to yourself, "Yeah okay? Umm... How do I know what's a sign and what isn't?"

Quickly then, your excitement unravels to disappointment as you realize the possibilities are endless. Eeek, sorry about that! Well hey, don't be bummed, we can work on that together. This is another reason why I hope you are working with a journal. There will be symbolism everywhere in that thing so make sure you read through everything that you write, especially a day or two later in case something pops up and forces you to take notice.

I can tell you that you just can't just ask the universe a question like, "Will I get this job?" Then run in your backyard looking for signs, see something jumping in the grass and be like, "Oh! I see a frog... must be a sign, let's Google what frog means."

You'd go bananas picking out everything around you and deciphering the symbolism behind them. Believe me it CAN be easy to get sign happy and start believing that the fly that just splattered on your windshield is an answer, too. Especially when you were thinking of nothing in particular. You really cannot be driving along, hear SPLAT, and go, "OMG spirit just sent me a sign I MUST see what that means." Or you could—but I think that's excessive and will get you nowhere fast.

Back to the frog. If he happened to hop into your lap or onto your sandwich when you were having a picnic, then it might be reason to scratch your head and say, "hmmm." If the fly suddenly landed on your windshield and stayed there during your trip or got sucked into your half open window and buzzed around your head the entire time, I would say that would be an excellent time to take notice.

Do you get what I'm saying here? Symbolism that comes through as a message for you is usually pretty obvious. It repeats itself until you yell up at the sky, "Ok! I get it!"

Chances are this has already happened to you and you just haven't really put two and two together. Or maybe you have and just refuse to believe it. Whatever you want to believe is entirely up to you, of course. You are allowed to be skeptical. Skepticism is good! Just don't let it completely impede on your progress.

The next thing you're probably wanting to know is, "how do you know what the symbols mean?"

If you want, you can do an internet search to begin with, or look it up in books. It may be really helpful to start that way actually, but you'll probably be frustrated when you find that different websites have different meanings for the same thing. In that case your best bet is to use the definition that feels right to you—yet another chance to use your intuition!

The best way, after you feel more comfortable and confident, is to figure out the meaning for yourself. As with the frog example, how do you feel when you think of or see a frog? Does it conjure up fond childhood memories or does it give you the heebies? Is there an old funny story associated with the frog? Does it spark nothing emotionally but you realize that the color green means something to you?

Think hard about the details of the symbolism you are receiving and write them down for later. If that poor frog indeed does give you the willies, don't take it as a bad sign, either. My guess is that it could have something to do with you getting over some sort of fear or uncomfortable situation, which is why that symbol was given to you.

I bet the last thing you wanted to ask me about was your **dreams**, wasn't it? Do me a favor and keep a whole other journal or tape recorder by your bed and record your dreams as soon as you wake up. You will be A-MAZED at what you recorded because you most likely won't remember it later in the day.

Remember my cough drop dream? I don't think I would have all the details as clear if I didn't write it down when I woke up. This includes middle of the night dreams too, as well as those moments of choppy sleep with a newborn or any kid who refuses their z's. You'll most likely have about three seconds to remember it so write it down the instant you wake up.

Don't worry about what you write, just blob it on the paper and go back to it when you can. I have had some amazing things happen when I've practiced dream journaling. I notice patterns, symbolism, and sometimes because of the recurring themes, can actually pinpoint what is causing the most anxiety in my life and then take steps to rectify the situation.

Of course not every dream will be a message or you might not be able to sort through the meaning no matter how hard you try. I've personally found that the more vivid the dream, the deeper the meaning. You'll figure it out as you go along and it certainly is fun to try!

Math Test

Just kidding. I'm absolutely awful at math. I just wanted to recap what we have learned.

1. Spirit and your subconscious communicates with you though symbolism.
2. Anything has potential to be a symbolic message for you. You recognize it by a distinct knowing, by repetition, or deja vu.
3. It is best to interpret the symbolism yourself when you feel confident enough to do so.
4. Dreams are fun! Write them down whenever you can and play around with what the different symbols in your dreams could mean.
5. Trust your judgement, don't chalk everything off to just coincidence.
6. Remain open and lighthearted in your endeavors to solve this very unique puzzle.
7. You will find answers to prayers, meditations, readings, open ended questions, etc. in this manner.
8. Try not to "over symbol" yourself. Signs and symbols usually repeat themselves or show up in ways that make you take notice.

From now on, pay attention to your dreams and to the little messages that pop up every day. See your world through spiritual eyes and know that the divine is all around you, communicating with you, all the time!

GROUNDED FOR LIFE

I knew when writing this book that one of the subjects I felt really deserved its own couple of paragraphs was "grounding"—as in how to ground yourself or why even bother. As I stared at the blank electric sheet of paper in front of me, I realized I couldn't figure out where to begin until I had the cutest flashback which is randomly relevant to the subject. (Thank you, Spirit!)

When my oldest was two years old or so I heard him yelling "Piggy, Piggy, Piggy!" in the little powder room by the front door of our house. Totally confused and fearing he had just drawn some sort of pig type creature on the wall, I hesitantly walked over. To my first bewilderment and then utter surprise, he was pointing to an electrical outlet!

How clever, I thought. *An outlet DOES look like a pig's snout.* I was just thankful he didn't have the foresight to try and stick some sort of metal instrument inside piggy's nose!

We lived in an older house where a lot of the electric wasn't updated so you would find a good number of outlets with two slots for a plug instead of three. In other words there was no grounding wire for many of them. Such was the case with my son's piggy outlet, or the aptly named, "pig-let" (hardy, har).

Let's talk electronics for a moment. What happens when you ground something that is electric? You complete a circuit to get rid of an electrical charge. If you are using an appliance that is plugged into the wall and it isn't grounded properly you have the potential to get quite a shock if something comes loose with the wiring because your body will end up being the next point for the current to go and get to the floor. YOU act as the ground and if this happens it will look like your local electric company is your new hair stylist.

Well that concludes your lesson on electronics today as that's pretty much as far as I go with knowledge on that subject. Now let's apply this to spiritual energy, shall we? Have you ever had one of those days when nothing seems to work out right? When your whole body seems to be out of sync with the rest of the world including yourself? It feels like your mind is floating away somewhere in the clouds and you are sort of seeing everything from a perspective that isn't your own. Usually this means that you aren't grounded, as in your energy isn't all inside your body or at all connected to the earth below you.

You're probably familiar with that whole spacey-floaty sensation I'm talking about but may be curious as to what can make you feel that way in the first place.

1. Lack of sleep.
2. Energy Vampires. (People who talk about themselves constantly and you feel soooooooo drained after hanging out with them.)
3. Spending too much time focusing on everyone else and not so much on yourself.
4. Not eating enough or eating improperly.
5. Full time caregiving.
6. Working long hours.

Of course the list goes on and I'm sure you get the idea by now that anything which could potentially drain your energy can cause you to become ungrounded.

Grounding is also important when embarking on a practice like meditation or using tools to develop intuitively. When you lead yourself on a meditation, your energy becomes raised and soon you can feel almost weightless, like you could easily be floating in the clouds. Without grounding yourself you could stay up in those clouds for the rest of the day. Okay ha ha you wouldn't REALLY be up there but it would sure feel like it.

Usually when you develop a spiritual practice you give yourself certain times to work and other times to be mundane doing all your earthly endeavors like fold the 3,000th pile of laundry and clean toilets and stuff. You want to make sure you are grounded or connected to the earth so you can be in the present, the here and now. Without it, your body will feel like it's floating away with your energy. Trust me on this! I've trial and errored around a lot of things.

How Do I Ground Myself?

1. Drink a glass of cold water.
2. Put your hands on the ground.
3. Hang on to some grounding crystals like hematite, onyx or jet.
4. Wash your hands.
5. Eat something.
6. Listen to your favorite music.
7. Go for a walk. Nature is the most grounding energy ever!
8. Imagine that you have roots growing out of the bottom of your feet (or tailbone where your root chakra is) and see/feel them shoot down into the ground anchoring themselves into the earth. <--That one is my favorite way to ground. If I'm feeling really saucy, after I send the roots out, I will imagine dark awesome earth energy coming back through the roots and up into my body to energize and center myself. Lots of fun this energy stuff is!

Before you begin any intuitive work, meditation, jump into a meeting or job interview, or get out of bed in the morning, try to ground yourself by one of the above mentioned ideas. Of course some will work better than others depending on the situation—use your own judgement and imagination. Keep track of your experiences in your journal.

See if you notice a change in your day by connecting with the energy we were born into. The earth!

WEEBLES WOBBLE BUT THEY DON'T FALL DOWN

It's true! Those Weebles never fall down. They just wobble and sway and end up right where they started. We could learn a lot from a Weeble.

Really though, do you know who is the most unbalanced person in the whole world? ME! I certainly have not been graced with the gift of sure footedness.

Here's a funny story: I spent a good ten and some odd years working in the entertainment industry. No no no, not the adult entertainment industry. Music and radio. Along with my hubby (who at the time was just the guy I crushed over at work) I produced and hosted a syndicated college radio show. It was a ton of fun and have come away with a million stories from that experience!

This one particular time we were staying in New York City for a few days to attend a college radio music conference. For this particular type of convention, there were bands scattered all throughout the city and you could easily whip around in a cab, subway, or on foot to almost any bar and know you were in for a spectacular show of musicianship. On this night, we were at a venue that had two floors and a balcony. I was all gussied up and feeling very self confident in my high heeled boots and cute punky outfit. The concert we were at was for a pretty popular group for college radio standards and the whole place was completely packed.

Me, being fairly short at a wee bit over 5ft tall decided to take the high road on the second floor so I could see the show better. I was all caught up in the euphoria of watching a good band and the vibe of the crowd you know, kind of like how you feel the first couple of days strolling outside with your new baby. That sort of pride like feeling takes over and just for a couple of minutes all is right with the world and you think self assuredly, "yeah.. I got this." Then of course the baby wakes up screaming and you are like 39 blocks from your house and you turn around and run in terror as you don't know where the hell you're going to whip out your boob or bottle to feed the wailing infant—and oh crap you also forgot diapers. Ha ha yeah, that was me this night. Except I didn't have a screaming baby (yet).

Standing at the very top of the steps at this full to the brim club, I looked out at the crowd dancing and singing, smoke swirling in the air as it does at such concerts. I felt like Rapunzel or Snow White up there on my little tower. I just needed cartoon birds to flutter past and a fairy godmother to save me from what happens next.

After a time, I decided to descend from my princess platform and find my coworkers down below somewhere and I. Missed. The. Top. Step.

Before I knew it, I was riding down about thirty steep concrete stairs half on my butt and half on my stomach as I tried to grab a railing on the way down and flipped over. As I got to the bottom, the only thing I could do was stand up, brush off and not look ANYONE in the eye. With head down, I whispered "I'm okay!" and walked as fast as possible to the other side of the room. It was a serious *Brady Bunch* movie Jan Brady moment. Sadly, that isn't the only one of my doozies but it's one of the funnier ones! I should have an unbalanced person of the year award framed and displayed on top of my piano.

As funny as that is, there is a point to why I shared my embarrassing story. Well actually, it has nothing to do with making a fool of yourself and more about explaining how important it is to keep yourself balanced. If I had kept my footing and paid attention to where I was going, I probably wouldn't have had to use my butt as a roller coaster cart down the stairs.

Similarly, if you keep an eye on everything around you. If you keep your mind focused on the present, with your feet on the ground and your hands to the sky, you will start to see that those nooks and crannies of life that you step into from time to time causing you to wobble won't make you fall. You may sway a little but definitely won't ride the stairs on your butt.

Maintaining Balance

This is actually a tricky subject because there is no tried and true method for this. Everyone ticks a little differently so one thing that works great for me may not work for you but I can at least try and point you in the right direction and let you figure out what works best from there.

A lot of the tools you see where is a good way to start. Through meditation, grounding and intuitive development, you can gain an aspect of spiritual balance (the hands in the sky part I mentioned earlier) but you have to keep your feet on the ground here on earth right?

1. **Scheduling.** Loosely plan your week and follow through even if you don't feel like it. Set aside a time every day when you pay special undivided (no phone, TV, internet or any other distraction) attention to your kids. If they let you, that is! Mine don't that often as they're usually way too busy playing and forcing them to hang out with me takes the fun and point out of the whole thing—so I usually have to take them out away from the house and the fun of the neighborhood. We go to a park without a playground because if there's a playground then they won't hang out with me there either. Nature walks work! You can take advantage of a big learning opportunity by talking about everything you see; all of the flowers, bugs, animals, season's changing, etc. If your kids are older then a stroll in nature could be a great grounding and balancing exercise for all.

If you are a very super hands on type of parent, schedule time for YOURSELF. Give the kids some independent activities and do something that you like to do. For you. Don't use the time to come up with meals for the week. Instead, read a non parenting book or magazine, create something, plant flowers, read the news (or maybe not…scary world) whatever it is that you did before kids, go do it for 15 minutes or so. I only say take the kids out of it because expending 100% of your energy on someone else can be extremely draining. Though as parents, we have to do that anyway, try like a bandit to create at least 15 minutes of time for you. You will find that you come out of it feeling refreshed, balanced, and ready to tackle all the fun stuff that kids throw at ya.

2. **Workaholic.** Some people work hard because they have to. Some have 3 + jobs a day to make ends meet, have kids to take care of, as well as everything at home. Others work a ton because they want to—like an addiction. If either of these scenarios are you, and you have the ability to take vacation or sick days, USE them. I know some who never take sick

days even though they have them and then lose them at the end of the year. USE the time to plan something, anything that isn't work related. Even if it's not a mini vacation. Maybe you want to catch up on housework, maybe you want to take the kids somewhere fun, whatever it is, and as long as it makes you happy, do it. Of course there are those situations where your work and social lives are one in the same and you really can't take a sick day. You owe it to yourself to take a break or two here and there. A 15 minute break at work to sit alone in the park outside with your shoes off (I totally just channeled a scene from *Pretty Woman*.) close the office door and meditate. What ever it is that floats your happy boat, even briefly, go ahead and do it. For you! You deserve it and it keeps you BALANCED.

The same goes for being a full time caregiver. Whether caring for children or others, steal a guilt free moment for you. Go and touch the ground, breathe deeply, reconnect with the earth, spirit, and yourself. Then go back in and rock that caregiving.

3. **Color/Art Therapy.** Sometimes something as simple as surrounding yourself with color or changing the colors around you can cause a mental, emotional, and/or spiritual shift and bring you back to contentment. I mention a little more about how color affects you in the section on meditation but it does a body good to physically add color to your world instead of just in your mind. If you are feeling down or "blue" try surrounding yourself with a bright sunny color like yellow or orange. Drink lemonade. (Ingest those colors!) Paint or use crayons with the kids and create something cheery. Mold with yellow play dough. Paint your walls! Do anything to add brighter color into your life.

If you feel particularly stuck in a certain situation look at your surroundings and the clothes you are wearing. See if you notice a pattern in regards to color. Are you constantly wearing the same shade of grey? Does your office wall glow that weird shade of white because of the fluorescent lighting that buzz's overhead all day long making you feel weird and dizzy? Adding a splash of color to the walls through a painting, a picture, or even a pretty colored Betta fish might be able to help!

We had a Betta fish named Sushi, in our office. I loved taking care of her every morning and she was always a conversation starter for clients. Colorful fish can really brighten up a place, as long as you take care of them, of course.

Do you see what I'm getting at here? Color has its own vibration and it can and does have the capability to change your mood which in turn can assist with balance. Don't be afraid to experiment and see where color can take you.

4. **Music.** Music is a huge part of my life. My husband is a musician. I worked in the industry for quite a few years. I grew up practically thinking the Beatles were somehow distant relatives of ours and can name pretty much any one of their songs (or belt out the chorus) just by hearing the very first note of a single Beatles tune on the radio. So it is no surprise that I surround myself with music to keep me balanced and sane. I have it on pretty much all the time at home, I answer people with song lyrics sometimes, and my guides send messages to my clients through song lyrics quite a bit when I'm doing readings for them. Music is such an integral part of my life. If it is yours as well, you might want to use it more as a tool for balance. If you're not a big music person then maybe try some mood music—like the dreamy new age stuff—or even Motorhead if that's your thing. Use whatever you think may be appealing and has the potential to calm and balance. Or maybe just turn off the radio or any noise and simply "enjoy the silence." <—see what I did there?

5. **Karma Chameleon.** Sometimes we simply need to shift focus away from ourselves and daily life and do something completely different. Actually this could also tie in to a learning opportunity for kids as well! Try volunteering at an organization to help out in your community. You could adopt a family around the holidays and have the kids help you prepare special gift baskets. You could adopt a soldier overseas and send them goodies from home that they're sure to be missing while away. If you are into animals, volunteer at an animal shelter but if you're anything like me or my kids, we would be bringing our friends home with us so choose your volunteer opportunities wisely. I bet a quick search online would bring up a bunch of different possibilities that you and/or your kids could get involved with.

If you have particular talents, use them! Visit a children's hospital or nursing home and share your talent with the patients to put a smile on their face. Volunteer to read a story. Be creative! Think about what could you do to help others. Big or small, it doesn't matter. It's just the doing that makes the difference.

Selflessly giving to others, in my opinion, is one of the highest forms of pure energy you can send out there. Eventually those good deeds will come back to you, showering you in return with love and assistance when you need it most. You would be on Santa's nice list for many years to come. :) Honestly though, helping others just FEELS good and may help to put your own life into perspective.

6. **Play and Laugh.** Laughter is one of highest forms of healing! Get outside with the kids and play, laugh, worry about nothing but the very present moment. Not only will you cherish that time with them and

vice versa, you will be practicing an active form of meditation! Learn to be completely in the here and now, don't worry about what happened earlier or what you have to do later. Gain your balance by being present and having fun!

7. **Meditate.** Ask spirit for advice during your meditations (examples later on). Try saying something like this during a meditation: "Help me find a way to balance my life with work, kids, etc." You may be pleasantly surprised at the epiphanies that pop into your head at any given time!

8. **Aromatherapy.** Whether through essential oils, incense, or the mouthwatering scent of a home cooked meal, surrounding yourself with your favorite scent is extremely grounding and therapeutic!

Another big thing that you can do to keep your life balanced is to look around and find the IMBALANCE. Take a look at your life and figure out what you spend the most time on. Think about what it is that you tend to dwell about the most. Write about it in your journal if you need to. Think about the whole situation and take note of how it makes you feel. If you notice that you are drained, depressed, anxious, irritable or some other unpleasant feeling, chances are your life isn't quite as balanced as it should be. Put the entire situation into perspective and figure out what you can do to change that. If you are spending way too much of your energy on one thing, carve out some time to shift your energy to something else for a little while. Even a small amount of time can do wonders.

I did this once! Okay, I've done this a few times in my life but this one is memorable. I'm going to give you a reading comprehension quiz right now. Think back to the very beginning of this book. Cough, cough INTRO SECTION cough, cough, cough. I bet you didn't read it did you? Well now you have to go back and read it to see what I'm talking about.

Okay, okay I'm not that mean, this is what happened in a nutshell. I'm not going to lie when I say that I had kind of a rough time emotionally when my kids were teeny tiny. I definitely think it was hormones, lack of sleep, and not being around a family unit (it really does take a village, as they say) which did me in for the first few months of parenthood. I was walking around like a zombie and had a random experience with hallucination in the middle of the night. One time during one of the many, many sleep deprived nights of my new mom-ness I turned over to pick up the baby when I heard him crying in his co-sleeper. When I did so, I was shocked to see a blonde haired curly headed baby hovering OVER the sleeper. Yes, yes I did. With a shake of the head and a quick rub of the eyes he was gone and I grabbed my real baby and fed him. Crazy, right?

The next night we had the rare opportunity for a date and went to a Van Morrison concert. He was supposed to be doing his live version of *Astralweeks*, one of my many favorite albums (cd's, records, downloads?) but he decided to experiment with new material first before he got into the part of the show that everyone came to see. The lights dimmed, the music began and in T minus 3, 2, 1 seconds I was out COLD. Hubby woke me up and took me out of there for dinner. We didn't even finish watching the show. Along the way to the exit, we passed a bunch of seated businessmen still in their suits. Their heads were drooped to the side, eyes closed, and mouths wide open catching flies. I think their happy hours ended too early and the no booze movement at the theater was a recipe for nap time!

Anyway, can't I ever tell a short story? Obviously I was not a balanced person by any means during this time period. So we did what any desperate Manhattan family would do. We hired a night nurse for a once per week. It took me the second time of her services to adjust to having someone else feed the baby at night, but when I caved and gave up my control, that one night of full uninterrupted sleep did WONDERS for my psyche and overall wellbeing. It's incredible how better you feel after you can some real rest.

Well there you have it, I was hugely imbalanced so we pinpointed the issue and tried to fix it. Well actually we sort of put a band-aid on it as I still wasn't sleeping during the week but I looked forward to that one single night of uninterrupted bliss!

***

If you can't quite put your finger on what your imbalance is, then another method to try is to shift your thinking. I know it is easier said than done in a lot of cases, but it really can be done if you try! In the very beginning of this book, I had mentioned that thoughts are things. If you are feeling energetically wonky—as in feeling physically, mentally, and/ or emotionally off and KNOW that it has nothing to do with a medical issue then it might help again to take a look at what's going on your life. Assess the entire situation and find out what it is that is making you feel that way. How do you FEEL when you think about certain areas of your current life? What is your attitude towards them? Is there a possibility that you are seeing all the negatives and none of the positives about what is going on? See if there is a way that you can flip your thinking about these situations. Try really hard to find the positives. If you catch yourself thinking poorly or negatively, try and let that go—then stick a positive, uplifting thought in its place. Do this for one week and see if it helps to shift the energy around you.

Of course, if you are in a very negative situation such as an abusive relationship, then thinking positive about the situation will not help. In this case, it's up to you to take action, speak to a professional and remove yourself from said situation. I'm talking typical every day human stresses and worries here. Not potentially harmful situations. Wisely use your own judgement, please.

There are many things that can make us feel off kilter. Look into your situation and figure out what you can do to wobble a little less and bring balance back into your life so that you can be a better parent, employee, employer, caregiver and human being.

PUTTING THE OM IN MOM

I find it ironic that right now I'm sitting in an airplane from Austin to Atlanta and it's pretty stormy down below causing us to rock around like we're sitting on top of a jello-mold. I love to travel but am admittedly not the best flyer, especially during flights like this! How appropriate then that I grabbed my laptop to write about meditation, as I had to remember to tell myself how to breathe!

Meditation is the art of silencing your mind so you can become aware of what exists internally as opposed to the outside world that you are constantly bombarded with. Meditation brings balance to your life, slows your heart rate down, chills you out when you think you're about to lose it, and allows for a few minutes to get away when it feels like there's no escape in sight or vacation days coming up. With it, you can find answers to problems that have puzzled you, gain spiritual insight, ground and center yourself for the day, help accomplish tasks that are ahead of you, have a small mental "vacay", or help others when you feel helpless. The benefits truly are overwhelming!

That's why I firmly believe that if you really want to begin the process of getting in touch with your spirituality, it might be time to start incorporating a little meditation into your routine.

Yes, I SO KNOW what you're thinking. There is no way that you have that kind of time to meditate. You barely have time to pee alone and I'm telling you to start a meditation practice. I'm not saying that you need to sit in a dark room cross-legged, staring at a candle for an hour. Although that would probably be very relaxing. That is until the kids came in, jumped on your back, blew out the candle, and asked you a million times to relight it so they can blow it out again and again and again. When you have a very busy lifestyle, it may just take some creative thinking on your part to get into the practice but it can be done and it is worth it. Believe me, if I can do it, anyone can!

Let's start right now by trying this exercise really quick…well not too quick, I don't want you to pass out or anything. So let's just say… two minutes. One minute, even…

Take a slow deep breath in through your nose. As you are slowly breathing in, mentally count to 6. I would say 10 but I just tried it and that seemed way too long for me. So the magic number here is 6. When you get to 6, hold your breath and count to 4. After that, exhale through your mouth. As you do count to six again.

Meditate:
1. Breathe in through your nose while counting to 6 (silently in your head).
2. Hold it for four seconds.
3. Breathe out through your mouth for a count of 6.

Try it a few times and see how you feel. It really shouldn't take you too long.

Now if you've managed to complete that exercise, then you just started the very basics of meditation. Good for you! And I bet while you were doing that, you weren't thinking about the kids, or work, or laundry, or whatever it is that you have to do, right? See! You've discovered one amazing reason why meditation is so beneficial.

Hide and Go Meditate

"Tiiiiiiime is on my side...yes it is!"

Why is something sung so passionately by Mick Jagger, the hardest thing to find? Time is typically not on the favorable side for busy parents so how can you manage to squeak in a few moments of uninterrupted bliss? (I'm not talking about sex here but there must be a book somewhere about how to balance that with parenthood. Seriously.) I mean meditation! As I said, you have to be creative when trying to shimmy in a few extra minutes—so to start your out-of-box thinking, here is a short list of ways that I have either tried myself or should have tried but didn't think about at the time. As you get more into your practice, you too, will find creative ways to steal a moment of zen or "borrow" rather, as it's bad ju ju to steal.

1. **In the bathroom.** Sitting on the potty is a great way to literally and figuratively release and bring balance. Yes, I'm in my thirties and just used the word potty. I am SO knee deep in baby hood. For the record, I'd sit on the toilet with the lid down first if trying to meditate in there.

2. **In the shower.** You can come up with wonderful cleansing types of meditations as the shower water falls over your head and cleanses your body. Simply imagine that the water is washing away all negativity and otherwise bad energy you don't need clinging to your body. See it in your mind or just know it is going down the drain. After you are "cleansed," imagine that the water coming down from the shower is of pure white light, restoring you from the outside in. Quick, and effective!

3. **When going to bed.** Deep breathing and visualization can be a fantastic way to drift off to dreamland. Before you do this, get a piece of paper and write down all the things you need to get done the next day so you don't have to worry about them when you are falling asleep.

4. **Waking up in the middle of the night.** I always meditate myself to sleep. Sometimes it makes for pretty interesting dreams. Deep breathing, visualizations, sometimes I have to count backwards from 500 if I'm really desperate. I don't get along well with numbers so I think I just get bored and fall back asleep. Again be creative and work with what you know about yourself.

5. Anytime of day or night when feeding the baby. To keep your sanity and strengthen the bond with your bundle.

6. Watching the kids play in the park. Just watching them is a meditation in itself, really. Also sitting on the grass, bench, in nature somewhere, or on a nice stretch of black top in the city— as long as you are outside in the sun and feeling the breeze, can be an amazing spiritual experience if you allow it.

7. Driving in the car. Prevents road rage! Just make sure you keep your eyes open and focus on breathing. Don't be closing your eyes and imagining pretty butterflies while your hands are on the wheel!

8. Lunch break. To regain balance during your work day.

9. Include the kids. If your kids are a bit older you can "try" incorporating them into your practice as well. It's a great "game" to play with them when you feel the energy needs to settle a bit in the room (ie. When they are driving you and/or each other bananas!) It's also a super sneaky way to squeak in your meditation as well as getting the kids to learn the importance of silence and quieting the mind. Better yet, have them close their eyes, take deep breaths, and picture their happiest memories.

When my guys were too small to really get the whole quiet thing, before they went to bed, we would play a game. I'd have them take a couple of deep breaths and then ask them about their happiest thoughts. Then I'd tell them as they're going to sleep to think only of their happy thoughts and listen to their breathing as they do it. One usually drifted off with no problem. The other, well… he's his own person that's for sure. If worse comes to worse, you can always play the "see who can be quiet the longest" game. I lose that one every time.

I know how difficult it is to start something new especially when you are probably spread so thin already, but if you can put forth the effort to cut a fifty calorie slice of time from your day for meditation, I bet in the not so distant future you will notice a change start to happen. You may not find that you have better abs but you'll probably witness a more relaxed body, mind, and spirit.

Which Style Is Right For Me?

I discovered meditation when I was ten years old. A little lady with a head full of massive white curls came into our fifth grade class with an old cassette player. She then turned the lights down low and told us to put our heads on our desks, listen to the music and relax. When I did as she instructed, within minutes I found myself floating away to some other place far away from the smell of pencil shavings and chalk dust. Every time she did this for us, I always had the same visual. I saw myself—quite a few years older—trudging through a harsh winter in a big city like Manhattan. I'd be stomping through a crowded sidewalk in the day time darkness that only a winter can provide. My wet feet would be splattering muddy slush and my head would face the ground to avoid the pelting snow. A split second later, I would be whisked away to some sort of mystical land seeking refuge from the storm.

Ironically, many years later, I actually did plod along through quite a few New York City winters just like the visions I had when I was ten. I've yet to visit the magical fairy place I saw but I'm pretty sure I can hold off on that one for awhile. Beyond that, I began to lead others in meditation to realms they too, escaped for comfort and solace. What a powerful thing guided meditation is! It's one of my fav's that's for sure. Aside from the guided kind though, there are also what seems like zillions of types of meditations styles: Buddhist, Zen, Transcendental, Mindful, Kundlini, Yoga, Zazen, and dozens more. Oh the fun you can have exploring, right?!

Keep in mind that you have to adapt to your style of learning when you do any sort of meditation. What I mean by this is that some people learn visually, while others are tactile, auditory, or incorporate some other way of using their senses to learn. I'm really not the best visual person. Even still, I've had some amazing visual experiences doing these types of meditations. What I realize though, is that a lot of the time, I'm really feeling the experience more than I am seeing what is happening. It may be the same for you or you could have a whole 3D movie playing out in front of you, or a musical even. The trick is to just go with it and let the experience be your guide.

In the following pages I have included a couple of simple meditation exercises for you to read over and try when time, and your creativity, grants. If you allow a few moments to squeeze it in, you may be pleasantly surprised by how balanced you feel. You could even be less frustrated, not so quick to anger, or simply notice that you are generally more balanced. Make sure to take special note of the positive changes you can make in your life with a few minutes of internal YOU time. Ultimately, I encourage you to explore as many forms of meditation that you wish and see what resonates best for you!

***

Tips and Tricks for Meditations:
1. Find a place where you will not be disturbed. (it may be easier than you think)
2. Relax, always relax.
3. Close your eyes, take a couple of deep breaths, and go in with absolutely no stress or expectations.
4. Do not force images, pictures, feelings or experiences to come while you are meditating. Relax and be guided.
5. Do NOT worry if nothing profound happens. It may be enough for you to just ease into the meditation and rest for a few minutes.
6. ALWAYS write down your experiences when you are done. Date the page, write down the type of meditation you tried, and ANY results. Do not dismiss anything. Write down how you felt, what you saw, heard, or even smelled. No matter how bizarre it may seem, write it down. Sometimes the strangest information provides the biggest message!
7. Make sure you ground yourself before and after.
8. Enjoy the experience!

Guided

I see guided meditations as sort of like a grown up version of story time. You can even hold your blankie while you practice! You or the instructor, if you are somewhere else besides your home, will read you a story which will allow you to close your eyes, relax, listen to the words, and go on a mental/spiritual journey.

I always tell my students that I'm guiding in class not to try too hard and never dismiss anything. If your mind wants to take you somewhere else that isn't being read during the meditation, then go where you are being lead. It is not gospel to follow the instructor's word. Simply feel what you are feeling and go with it! (another valuable lesson with spirituality) I once had dismissed my results as having an overactive imagination to which my peers in class said, "no way... in meditation there is no such thing as imagination." Those words really resonated with me. Just as vivid dreams are chalk full of symbolism, so too is meditation. After you are finished always write down your experiences in your journal. You may be amazed at the information that you uncover or the insight that you gain.

Guided meditations can be done in a couple of different ways. One thing you can do is to go out and find a workshop in your community somewhere that does them. Often times you'll see your local bookstore, new age shop, yoga studio, or even some churches holding them weekly, monthly, or daily. If it's too hard for you to get out, you can scour the internet for websites like iTunes, YouTube, or online stores to download and listen at your leisure.

In the case of this book though, I'm going to write out the meditations in list format. I encourage you to read through it once and either see if you feel like remembering everything or to grab a tape recorder or the voice recorder on your smart phone. Record yourself reading through the list very slowly, pausing a few seconds between each number, and then playing it back so you can relax and enjoy the meditation. If either option doesn't work for you, you can always close your eyes, get yourself as relaxed as you possibly can, then read the first instruction on the list. Close your eyes again, take the time you need to follow whatever you were asked to do, open your eyes again, read the second instruction and so on. It's not totally ideal BUT it does work and will get you to that dreamy relaxed state that we all love about meditation.

For your very first guided meditation, I thought it would be fun to start with one that I wrote years ago called "Tree and Seed." Before you begin, think about what you would like to bring into your life. It could be anything at all—just something that you want to manifest for yourself. Maybe you want a new car, better job, less stress, to be at peace, or any thousands of possibilities. Take a minute right now and think about it. It can become as simple or complex as you want, just remember to let your mind go and not worry about where your thoughts lead you.

Lastly, make sure your journal is somewhere close by so you can write about your experience as soon as it's done. Now go relax and enjoy!

Tree and Seed

1. Make sure you are comfortable, close your eyes and take a couple of deep breaths.
2. As you breathe in, think the word relaxation.
3. As you breath out, imagine you are letting go of all your worry and stress.
4. Breath in and out.
5. Uncross your arms and legs and relax every single muscle.
6. Feel your feet on the ground and know that you are connected to this room and the earth.
7. Relax.
8. Imagine that you are somewhere out in nature. You are safe and secure. The temperature is perfect for you here.
9. Make a mental note of what your surroundings look like. What can you see? What can you hear? What can you feel?
10. You notice that next to where you are standing is a shovel. You pick it up and start to dig a shallow hole into the earth. While you are digging you are surprised at how effortlessly you can do this!
11. After you feel that you are done digging, you put down the shovel and notice a package containing one seed laying on the ground. Pick it up and put the seed in your hand. What does it look like? Is it small? Is it large? What color is it?
12. In your heart you know that this seed is a vessel that holds a single wish that you have for yourself. Take a moment now to think of a wish—something that you truly want in life.
13. Hold the seed in your hand and speak your wish out loud.
14. Now plant the seed in the hole that you dug.
15. Say your wish one more time when you are done planting. Your wish is like water to the seed, all that it needs to grow is your intention!
16. Step back and watch it grow!
17. Do you notice anything coming out of the earth? What is growing from the seed that you planted?
18. After your wish is done growing, spend a few minutes looking at and reflecting on it.
19. Take another minute to breath deeply and say thank you for the message, if any, that you received.
20. Take a few more deep breaths then come back into the room you are sitting in. Feel your feet on the ground, know that you are home.

21. Open your eyes and start writing about your experience. Try not to stop and think about it. Just write, write, write. Or talk into the voice recorder about what happened.

      What did you think about that guided meditation? I really like the tree and seed scenario because it puts a solid visual onto your dreams and helps you to start manifesting in your mind and in the realm of meditation instead of here on our physical plane. I think that is important because a lot of us believe our wishes and dreams as insignificant or unrealistic. In the ethereal realm, there is no room for ego. No dream or wish is too big or too silly as long as it comes from your heart and with the best of intentions in mind. Don't forget that the place where you go to in dreams and meditations are worlds full of symbolism. So if your wish grew and turned into a giant oak tree or Marilyn Monroe then that's okay! Just think about what that symbolism could mean to you personally, or cruise the internet for symbolic thought starters.

      You may just have gotten some clues or insight from your guides or your spiritual self. Sometimes we already have the answers to our questions, we just need to clear the clutter from our hearts and minds to get there! Meditation helps!

White Light

"Run to the light, Carol Anne, Run as fast as you can!" Diane Freeling yelled desperately to her daughter in the first *Poltergeist* movie. The whole "light' scenario use to confuse me because they told that poor little girl to go into the light, stay away from it, and then go back in. I don't know about you but that kinda made my head spin. I thought of that scene as I started contemplating the role that white light plays in spirituality. The light I will be referring to, however, will not surface in your closet and serve as a portal to another dimension. This particular meditation is a helpful tool for protection, manifestation, and balance.

So what's the deal with white light anyway?

While I don't know a whole lot about the science of color, I do know that each color vibrates at its own unique frequency. And when you breakdown white sunlight through a prism, you see all the colors of the rainbow. In essence, that must mean that white light should be an extremely high vibration if it contains all of the colors within itself.

Taking that knowledge and mix it with the idea that simple thoughts can become tangible things (energy flows where thought goes) and you have white light meditation.

Centuries worth of spiritual people have used the idea of surrounding themselves with white light to protect themselves from bad spirits or unwanted energies. Many consider white light to vibrate at the same speed as the divine or angels. Look at any old spiritual painting and you will see that many of the subjects are surrounded by some kind of white light or halo. They even portrayed that idea in the movie, *Sixth Sense* where every picture of the little boy had some sort of bright light behind him.

So how can this whole concept help you? Easy! Using white light in meditation can help you to focus, to change your awareness to something positive, manifest the transformation you want to see in yourself, provide spiritual protection, get answers to burning questions, as well as to enhance your well being. Sounds crazy, I know—but it's true. Besides, what harm can be done by a little positive thinking?

The reason why questions can be answered during meditation is because you've managed to quiet your mind from outside influences allowing you to start thinking more clearly. Some would also say that it's a method of raising your vibrations so you can receive messages from your guides, angels, or your understanding of the divine. I will leave the theories up to you to decide for yourself, but know that no harm can come to you by allowing yourself time to unwind.

The next meditation I created for you is a very simple one to help you explore the white light energy and see how it feels. It's not so much as a guided meditation as it is an introduction. I suggest that you read through the steps I've outlined on the following page and see what feels best for you. Experiment with what I have written out or create your own way to work with it. As always, write down your experiences and go in without stress or "doing it right." Enjoy and have fun!

Simple White Light Meditation

1. Sit somewhere quiet if possible.
2. Close your eyes.
3. Take a couple of deep breaths.
4. Imagine that a bright white light is surrounding every part of your body, like a shell or bubble of comfortable, healing energy. You could also imagine it coming down from the sky through the top of your head permeating every part of your body as it makes its way to your toes, out of your feet, and into the ground.
5. If you can't really "see it" because you're not very visual, try to feel it surrounding you. Or just tell yourself it's there and know that to be true.
6. While you're surrounded by this light, you can simply bask in the knowledge that you are protected and your energy is vibrating in such a way that no harm can come to you. You can sit and silence and listen to the blissful nothingness or you can use this time to listen to your inner voice and get some answers.
7. Hold this notion of the white light filling your inner and outer being until you feel you are done.
8. Come back into the room, feel your feet on the ground, your butt on the chair, or generally have the knowledge that you are grounded and back into your room.
9. Open your eyes, and write or talk out your experience.

***

I find that this meditation can be particularly useful in the middle of a workday when you're swamped and feel like you're starting to lose focus.

You can also use a variation of this meditation to bring other positive changes. Say you really want a new job and nothing's coming up for you. Imagine yourself doing the job that you dream to do and surround it with white light feeling or stating the true intention of bettering yourself and keep working towards that goal. It will help you to get there.

You can also send white light to a situation that typically causes a certain level of anxiety for you. In my case it would be a public speaking event or a blood test. In meditation, I would imagine myself giving my speech or at the lab getting my blood drawn. I'd try and see as much detail as I possibly could and then imagine the room that I'm in, everyone with me, and myself are saturated in white light. It truly helps by sending confidence and protection to yourself on the spiritual plane and surprisingly makes you feel a little more calm on the actual day of the event.

Isn't it nice knowing that you have this endless supply of universal love and support?!

You can surround your friends and family with it for blessing or protection. Surround people or situations that you don't particularly care for. It's good practice to stop sending negative, harmful thoughts because what you send, you get back! Sending the good as well as the bad situations positive energy may help expedite the process of healing on an even greater level because of the higher vibration of positive energy. Remember the movie, *Monsters, Inc*? Laughter was WAY more powerful than unhappy screams, right?

Oh and in work or social situation, Mentally surrounding yourself with white light can help to keep your energy to yourself when you come across that person that talks waaaay too much and leaves you drained. You know what I mean?

So there you have it. White Light. You don't need a whole hour or half hour to incorporate this practice into your life. Just a few minutes or moments of silence is all it takes and the possibilities are endless. Give it a try!

Walking

Walking meditations can teach you mindfulness, help you to develop further spiritually by being in the present moment, increase energy, and improve concentration. The best part about it is that it can be done just about anytime and anywhere. All you need is your own sacred body and motivation. It can be a little tricky with kids in tow, but I used to just hold the smaller one and have the other one practice with me. See...anything is possible!

Let's pretend the weather is decent and we're outside at a park or on a nature trail. (This can be done walking from your car to work, on a busy sidewalk, in your house, wherever. Let's try not to limit our potential. Keep the creative mind always open.) As you're walking, focus on your breathing for a couple of minutes. Make sure you are walking at a pace that doesn't take your breath away.

Steps for Steps
1. Pay attention to your feet. Tell your left foot you need to step. Feel yourself pick up your foot and place it on the ground. Then do the same with your right foot. Or do it the other way around if you feel weird starting on your left foot.
2. Feel the soles of your feet as they touch the earth. Be completely mindful that you are walking with intention.
3. As you walk, see if you can sync your breathing with your footsteps. Don't force it. Step with your right foot as you inhale. Step with your left and exhale. Or see how many steps it takes you to naturally go through one cycle of inhalation and exhalation. Be mindful of your breath. Be mindful of the steps you're taking.

This is a great exercise to help you learn to stay in the present moment so you can not dwell on the past or worry about the future. Just focus on your intention to walk and see how easily your body responds.

As you get more used to this type of meditation, try pretending that as your feet touch the earth, they are sending little hugs or blessings to the ground. As your foot lifts, imagine a flower, plant, or berries growing from the spot in the earth where you left your blessing. This is a good spiritual exercise for giving back and sending positive energy. When I say giving back, I mean, giving back to the earth because its our home. Give back to the natural world in which we all share helps us to further appreciate this beautiful world that we live in.

You can also start using the energy you are creating by walking to focus on goals you wish to achieve, sending prayers out to people, forgiving yourself and others, or just being completely and totally yourself in the present moment.

It only takes the right intention to create the best possible life for yourself! Go ahead and give it a try. Try it when you are circling the living room with your colicky baby. Take a brief stroll to another desk at the office. Make it count. Every moment is a gift or "present."

Spirit Being

Hi my name is Jen Brunett and I'm a Reiki master and natural intuitive. Cringe, cringe. I don't like to label myself. Plain ol' Jen Brunett works just fine for me. I'm not a big fan of labels and titles but I suppose they are as much apart of life as…well…oxygen really. We all have names, job titles, job titles on top of those job titles or otherwise describe ourselves by level of degree and/or certifications.

I mean look at me. Reiki Master. Sure, I've taken the proper certifications and have been a practitioner for over a decade but I certainly don't feel I've "mastered" it. Reiki is a practice and I learn and evolve through each and every client, study, or workshop I attend, as well as daily self-treatment. (With Reiki you have the unique advantage of giving yourself treatments.) Yes, I have acquired the title of Master because of my level of certification but I feel as though I'm a constant work in progress as we all are. We all have this tendency to define ourselves by WHAT we are, not WHO we are.

And who exactly are we? "We are spiritual beings having human experiences." Someone told me that a long time ago and it totally resonated—kind of filled in the void of all the unknowns in life. It was the line that connected some of the dots that I had trouble seeing.

Of course we're human but isn't that a label, too? So what does it mean to be a "spiritual" being? The Dictionary describes spirit as "the principle of conscious life; the vital principle in humans, animating the body or mediating between body and soul."

There's a force within us that goes way deeper than I believe most of us understand, myself included. Our human-"being" is trained to believe in things that can be seen, measured, and dissected. Our spiritual-"being" thrives on intuition, natural instinct, authenticity and love.

The meditation to follow, therefore, is not a mantra, a verse, or a guided walk through the woods. It is homework to find out what lies inside the very core of your essence, to see yourself as a spiritual being.

Spirit Being Meditation

Imagine all of your material possessions being stripped away. This would include: your college degrees, driver's license, Prada bag, smartphone, home, Keurig, anything and everything that that you cannot live or be without. Go ahead and do that right now and try not to panic, just seriously give it a few seconds to let the scenario I've just laid out for you to sink in.

Would you disappear too? No you wouldn't. But you might feel like you want to! What's left after everything in your world is taken away? YOU. Pure and natural YOU. With your human shell and your heart free to roam. Vulnerable, maybe. Refreshed and energized, most likely.

Now you have the opportunity to really figure out what you want and need since you've already experienced all the things that have been taken away. Do you really need them back? Really? Okay, your house maybe, but what about all the clutter inside of your house? Do you honestly need that one dusty pair of shoes from the 80's or 90's? I could ramble here, but the thing I ask is to try and imagine it. See what looking into your spiritual being can do for you and for those around you. Write or even draw out your experience in your journal.

Sounds of Silence

Can you imagine unplugging from everything for just a couple of minutes each day? That means your phone, computer, iPad, iPod, Wii, television and whatever other type of stimulating electronic exists out there. How about unplugging from the constant buzz of people noises in your house or office? How about disconnecting the inner chatter of your own mind? You know, that constant conversation you have with yourself about what you need to do, how to get it done, and what comes next?

Being quiet is a truly therapeutic and inspiring meditation. Believe it or not, it really doesn't have to take a lot of time but it does require a little effort on your part. It might take sheer will and determination to walk away from all the noise and distraction and perhaps a bit of a struggle to find a creative place to give it a try.

I have one solution that may sound silly but it's sure to give you a couple of free minutes no matter where you are. Ready for this? The bathroom! When you have a busy lifestyle, the bathroom is one of the only places you can be quiet and still for a small amount of time. Am I right?

Here's what you need to do:

Don't take anything with you but yourself. Close the door. Put the toilet lid down and sit. Breathe. Think of being in the present moment. Think of silence, think of nothing. If a thought pops in, just let it go. Tell yourself you need a few minutes to reboot. Which, in all reality, is exactly what you're doing here. You are rebooting your mind, body, and spirit.

If you have your phone or computer on for days without restarting, what happens? Applications get left on that bog down your system. Sometimes errors start popping up and updates don't show on websites. It is the same thing with your mind in a sense. If you are constantly on the go and don't give your mind a break you can go on overload too!

Like I said, it doesn't take long, a simple few extra minutes each day of mostly total silence and complete nothingness is all you need. Focus inward, focus on the present, on how grateful you are to have that moment to be alone and to reboot. Give silence a try and see how rejuvenating it can be!

Meditation is a tool that we, as busy parents and beings, can utilize for bringing balance into our hectic lives. It helps us to stay in touch with our spirituality, escape for a few moments, and breathe deeply which is uber important for healing and to quell anxiety. You will find more meditations in upcoming pages that pertain to the subjects featured as well. I'm such a huge fan of it, I couldn't help to sneak it in wherever I could. I hope that something you find within this chapter will assist you by bringing internal balance or perhaps spark some research to discover other types of meditations that call to you.

It's time to put the Om in Mom!

WALKING ON SUNSHINE

I can't help but to tie part of this Chapter into Reiki as most of my experience in the chakra and aura department have to do with my being a Reiki practitioner. Truth be told, I didn't quite totally believe in chakras, auras and all that stuff until I started working with Reiki even though I had always yearned to see those things for myself.

One time I went to this outdoor wellness/spiritual festival and I wanted to be just like this lady that I saw in the vendors area. She was wearing an electric colored tie dye t-shirt and her hair was overgrown like an unattended back yard hedge. I watched as she would bark out the names of colors to every person that passed by her little booth as though her attempts served as a vocal pamphlet for her psychic energy reading business. Some people stopped to talk and others gave her the stink eye. I wondered if she really could see people's chakra and aura colors. I was too shy to ask her and still very skeptical.

That summer, I started reading the *Celestine Prophesy*. On sunny days (which can be rare where I live) I would lay in the grass and stare at my hand raised towards the sky using the white clouds as a backdrop, trying like hell to make out an energy pattern, shape, or color that was supposed to be emanating from my hand or fingers, like they did in the book. I never saw a thing. I was disappointed and eventually convinced myself that those members of the old spiritual traditions I have been reading about must have been completely hopped up on the cactus juice to see all these amazing visions that they had been writing about for centuries.

I'd love to tell you brilliant stories of my seeing beautiful swirling colored halos of auric delight around every person I've met since babyhood. Sadly, that just isn't the case. I obviously wasn't always one to believe through faith alone, though I have done a lot of self-improvement in that department since. It wasn't until I attended a meditation class in my late teens/early 20's that I had my first real experience with the energy of chakras, auras, and the power of what balancing those puppies can do!

At the time I was in school and working (story of my life) and things were particularly stressful for whatever reason. I was also going through the highs and lows of panic disorder and depression.

There was a meditation class every Tuesday night that I would attend with nine or ten others in an attic of a store that was converted from a house in the city. I just recently found out that it's actually still going on now but it's in another town. (Mental note…must make a pilgrimage!)

In this class, sometimes we would do a short meditation, other times we didn't. The woman who led the classes, Dr. Frances Carns, is an amazing intuitive medium, reputable healer, and would tell thought provoking stories about her life, have us do spiritual exercises, and whatever else she was prompted to do at the moment. It was a lot of fun and very eye opening for me at the time.

At the beginning of one class in particular she had asked us if we wanted her to do a little Reiki for us. I sat in curious silence with a question mark over my head as excited "ooohs" and "yes, pleases" filled the rest of the room. Apparently I had missed a previous class where she had done this…thing…before.

I honestly can't remember how she explained it or if she even did but there was a chair in the middle of the room and the center of the circle our little group had made. One by one a person would get up to sit in it and wait for her to do the "ray thing" or whatever. When she rested her hands lightly on a person's head they would say things like, "your hands feel hot" or "I can feel that" when she wasn't touching them at all, her hands would hover a few inches from their shoulders or forehead. She would also tell the person she was "working" on any psychic information she picked up and people rotated out every five minutes or so.

Even though I've been going to these classes for awhile and really liked and trusted the instructor, I was a little beside myself with skepticism. I had no idea what was going on and couldn't believe that people could "feel" anything.

What did that even mean?

As my turn came, I was very interested but a little nervous. I didn't know how to act or what I was supposed to feel. Wide-eyed and somewhat reluctant, I slumped into the chair in the center of the room.

The first thing she said to me was, "Your third eye is crooked."

Eh? I thought.

Before I could verbally raise a question, she put her hand up to the middle of my forehead, made a fist, then grabbed the air and motioned away from my body like she was pulling a rope out of my head. Seriously!

And you know what? My whole head jerked forward like I DID have a rope coming out of the middle of my forehead! Then she put her hands up and lightly touched the sides of my face and said, "this is for your confused thoughts," and I felt the heat around my ears which seemed to come directly from her palms—and that was the end of it. As I sat back down on my beanbag, I could still feel the heat on my face like I had just walked off with her warms hands planted firmly over my ears, a phenomenon I'm now very familiar with that we Reiki people like to refer to as "phantom hands."

As I left that meditation class, I allowed my first Reiki experience to melt away and opened the door to let in normal life and stress. It wasn't until I woke up for work the next day that I understood what Reiki and chakra balancing actually does.

When I sat up from bed after turning off my alarm I immediately could tell something was different, but I couldn't place it. It started to click for me while I was in the car when I was dealing with the worst morning commute ever! Being stuck at a red light for an absurd amount of time it dawned on me that I wasn't frowning and swearing at the traffic light. I had the radio on full blast and was bouncing around, singing. Thank goodness it was winter-time and the windows were up because no ones ears need to be graced with my unpleasant singing voice…especially that early in the morning. I could make people's hot drinks spill over as even the coffee would try to get away from the horrible sound.

I was happy. Like really happy. Giddy even. As I arrived at work and went about my day, this feeling stayed. At the time, my office was in a basement with no windows (think *Joe Versus the Volcano*). On this day, it felt lighter down there, brighter even, and I sat down at my desk with a big silly smile. I picked up the phone to call Dr. Carns to tell her how I felt and ask just what the heck it was that she did to me.

She just said, "Well that's Reiki!"

Crazy. Why can't they bottle this stuff to drink every morning? The world would be a much happier place! I knew right then that it was something I wanted to do for myself and possibly for other people. I couldn't imagine keeping this thing a secret.

Fast forward maybe two years after my initial experience. I found a Reiki master I trusted and learned it for myself. Even though my experience lead me to practice Reiki, you don't have to go that route unless you feel drawn to it, there are other ways to balance your chakras on your own.

The biggest ways are through my favorite, meditation, the use of tools such as a pendulums or crystals (you can learn more in the chapter on intuition), surrounding yourself with colors that correspond with your chakras, yoga, or to go and see a trained energy worker such as Reiki, Qi Gong, Integrated Energy Therapy, Angel Therapy, etc. There's a long list of people more than willing to help you to keep your weeble from wobbling, just make sure that you do your research first and find someone that's reputable. Word of mouth is usually the best way, in my opinion.

Wheels of Fortune

After that initial experience with the forehead rope to which I now know was my third eye chakra, I've made it a point to try and keep them in check as often as I can. Also, with every Reiki client I have, I focus on balancing their chakras as well and we always discuss and take note of any subtle changes they may have felt during their treatments.

So have I lost you yet? Are you sitting there wondering what the heck am I babbling about? If you're new to the business of chakras and auras I'm sure you've at least heard the name before and probably associate it with some crazy eastern meditation thingy... or something. Although our society is just becoming hip to the art of using these little buggers for balancing our minds, bodies, and spirits, people in the eastern part of the world have had this knowledge for like, ever! And let's face it, if we can start the morning or end our day with a little balancing instead of (or along with) "mommy's little helper" (insert booze of choice...ha ha) then we might just make it through early mommy-hood with less grey hair, worry lines, heart palpitations...

Chakra is the Sanskrit (Eastern Indian) word for wheel. We each have a series of these wheels that run along the mid line of our bodies. Where on the body, exactly, seems to be somewhat debatable. Some people say that the seven main chakras run along the spine, others say that five of the seven run along the spine and the other two are on the front. There are even other variations just to confuse you more! I think personally that they run right through your body, front and back and affect the organs, glands, and muscles on each side.

Think of your chakras like little tornados or spinning vacuums, not unlike a black hole out in the galaxies. Each is assigned a color which has its own vibration (as color does) and affects a certain part of your body as well as your overall physical, mental, and emotional well being. Each chakra essentially contains a blueprint of your life. These vortexes are affected by the environments you've been in, the people you've been around, and the emotional states that you've felt since you first made your entrance here on earth. Essentially, they KNOW how you roll in life, and cater their subtle energy to your specific needs.

Sometimes an illness, poor emotional state, improper diet and other factors can throw them off balance which would affect the organ or bodily system closest to that chakra as well as your mentality. Once all chakras are balanced, it allows your energy to flow throughout your being creating a harmonious environment for your mind, body, and spirit.

For example, previous to when my meditation instructor rebalanced my third eye chakra, I was feeling closed off and anxious. The day after she worked her mojo, I felt open an alive! I believe that along with my third eye, it probably affected my solar plexus as well because chakras like to work together. Your third eye is famously noted for its connection with clairvoyance but it also stands for your perception in regards to how you view yourself and the world around you. Me, being particularly shy, was very drawn into myself and had a third eye too closed or wonky to allow myself to experience anything other than what was going on in my own head. In other words I would over think myself into a panic attack.

If my solar plexus (the seat of personal power) was closed, then for sure I would feel powerless against all the people that I come in contact with every day. I believe through balancing these two chakras, I was able regain my personal power and come out of my dark shell of timidity to experience and bask in the proverbial and literal sunshine.

I know this sounds all hocus-pocus but it really transformed me. Once you start working with your own chakras you will see a difference within yourself and the world around you as well. Don't be discouraged if it isn't completely life changing right away. I believe the universe needed to give me a huge energetic kick in the rear, which is why it happened for me the way it did. It may only be subtle adjustments for you, but it WILL create whatever change needed that is perfect just for you.

Life in Color

I've already mentioned that you can seek out the aid of an energy worker or start a yoga practice to help balance your chakras. You can also do this on your own through meditation. I've written a simple meditation for you try since you have all that extra time. (wink, wink) A good way to sneak this in might be just before you go to bed at night or even in the shower! The bonus about the shower is that as you are working with your chakras you can imagine that the water is cleansing more than the mushy baby peas that were thrown into your hair. The water is also washing off any negative energies that have infiltrated and became stuck in your energy field throughout the day.

This meditation might be hard for some as it requires a certain amount of visualization. If you can't see the color, perhaps you can visualize a food, flower, or baby food jar, with matching color properties. If that doesn't work then try to feel with your intuition where this chakra is or simply acknowledge out loud and know in your heart that each one is balanced and so it will be! Remember when I said that thoughts are things?

Here is a handy list of the chakras, their colors, and meanings for reference before you begin the meditation and/or any ol' time you need a reminder.

ONE. ROOT. RED.

Your Root Chakra is located in the area of your perineum. If you had a vaginal birth you'll know this area as the one that sang the song "Ring of Fire" or the cause of you not being able to sit down for weeks after because of all the darn stitches. If you had a c-section or haven't delivered yet, you'll know it as the spot where you squeeze sooooo hard to keep your pee from escaping even though you just went to the bathroom 5 minutes ago. If you've never experienced pregnancy, then it is the spot down below where you squeeze muscles while doing the pee pee dance.

Your root is responsible for keeping you grounded, stable and connected to the energies of the earth. Those days when you are about to fly off the handle…it would be a good time to think about balancing your root chakra.

TWO. SACRAL. ORANGE.
Your Sacral Chakra can be found below your belly button and above your pubic bone. Many people know this one as the root of your sexual functions. If you aren't feeling so randy anymore (not terribly uncommon when you are covered in poop and baby puke half of the day and sleep a whopping three hours at night) then this is the chakra to focus on for balance. It is also your energy center for relationships, passion and creativity.

THREE. SOLAR PLEXUS. YELLOW.
Your solar plexus hangs out just above your belly button and below your rib cage. This is the seat of your personal power, your will, and ego. Balancing this guy can definitely help you feel more confident about your place on this beautiful green rock of ours.

FOUR. HEART. PINK/GREEN.
You can guess where this chakra is located and I bet you would be right! The heart energy encompasses everything that you would assume that it would (love, compassion, trust). But it also talks about self love and your connection to those around you. Sometimes we feel cut off from people that we love, they just don't understand us or we don't understand them. That type of feeling can spawn from a heart chakra that is imbalanced.

FIVE. THROAT. LIGHT BLUE.
Your throat chakra sits at the base of your throat, above your collar bones and below your Adam's apple. It is the center of communication. I usually find I have to focus on this more often than the others as I always feel tongue tied and manage to squeak out the wrong set of words. It also harbors feelings of fear where communication is concerned.

SIX. THIRD EYE. DARK BLUE/INDIGO.
Your third eye is at the center of your forehead, just above the junction of the eyebrows. Whether or not you are familiar with chakras, most have heard of the "third eye" and its notorious definition for being responsible for psychic insight. It definitely is the seat of your visual intuition. Its energy also represents greater wisdom and inspiration.

SEVEN.CROWN. PURPLE/WHITE.
The crown chakra sits at the top of your head and is your direct connection to your understanding of the divine. It represents your higher self, spiritual clarity and your accepting of a higher power. When you want to communicate with god/great spirit/the universe, try to meditate

on opening your crown chakra and see if you notice a feeling of greater connectedness.

Simple Chakra Meditation

1. Start by closing your eyes and taking a couple of deep breaths.
2. Try and relax as much as possible.
3. See the color red in front of you. If you can't see the color, maybe imagine a red rose or other flower, or see a bright beautiful red apple.
4. Take a deep breath and as you do so, imagine that you are breathing this color into your lungs. Feel it go through your body into your root chakra. Know that you are grounded, protected, and safe and that your root chakra is now spinning a bright and vibrant red. It is perfectly balanced.
5. Repeat the same steps with chakras 2-7: Orange, yellow, green, blue, purple. See, feel, and know that your chakras are all in balance and working together to create a strong vibrant energy foundation for yourself so that you can be the best and most comfortable and confident person that you can be.
6. Say a small prayer to your understanding of the divine stating that you are balanced. Ask for their protective light to surround you now so that you may stay in perfect balance throughout the day. As always, a little thank you couldn't hurt at the end. Gratitude is humbling, powerful, and healing.

**

With practice you'll know this meditation by heart and will be able to find your own creative ways to incorporate it into your day. Hopefully this lights within you a curiosity that will lead you to further study the subject as everything I've written here is just a teeny tiny sliver from an old redwood tree. I really just want to lay down the foundation and if you find that you like working with your chakras to bring balance, I wish you the best of the best on your studies!

May your future be lined with color!

GUIDES AND ANGELS

I've tossed and turned over this chapter for awhile now, and even though you see this subject quite early on, I didn't include it until after the rest of these pages were done and edited. I think the biggest reason for my hesitation is because I really want you to understand that our spiritual world is not a particle of imaginary dust, it is a living and breathing creation which expands with us as we continue to learn, develop, and grow.

Some people embrace the idea of spirit guides, angels, or some other form of "spiritual helper," while others will not dare to dip a toe in and feel the other worldly waters. Either reaction is completely valid, it is YOUR journey, after all. After reading through this manuscript, I realized that I mention spirit guides and angels quite a bit and since I personally love talking to and working with my own guides, I've decided to dedicate this very chapter to them. If this is a subject that is too far fetched for you then please skip and move on to other parts that suit you. I do encourage you to come back when you feel comfortable and read through with an open mind when you are ready!

**

I often get asked about spirit guides when I give Reiki treatments because of the spiritual nature of the practice, I suppose. During one session in particular, I told my client that there was someone in spirit around her with an "N" name. My client then told me that she recently went to an intuitive that said she had a spirit guide named Nancy hanging around her. She told me she didn't know she even had a spirit guide and had no idea that they were there.

A lot of people don't realize it but everybody has a "spiritual helper." Some people call them angels, others call them guides or even totem animals (Native American tradition) as your teachers don't always have to be human!

A spirit guide is not unlike our understanding of a Guardian Angel, which I've found, most people have a more comfortable association with. In fact, I believe the two to be interchangeable concepts in some ways. For the sake of ease, let's say that they are one and the same. I'll bet you have your own personal angel story or know someone that does! I've heard an awesome amount of angel stories myself, ranging from healing and answered prayers to night time visits and near death experiences.

Speaking of which—something happened to once, that I'll never forget. This particular day as an almost twenty something and going though that awkward time period where I hadn't gotten the whole, "I need food for sustenance so probably had popcorn for breakfast and no lunch" kind-of-thing down yet. I went to my doctor's appointment being noticeably starving and very apprehensive knowing I had to get a blood test. (I have horrible needle phobia.)

After the big poke in the arm, I remember feeling kind of weird. I told the nurse how I felt and she told me that I didn't look pale or anything. Becoming more green by the second, I sort of yelled in response,

"Well I FEEL pale!"

Deciding that something MUST be going on, she whisked me over to the examining table to lay down. I looked up at the random, ripped at the corner, magazine picture of a forest taped to the ceiling and then my lights went out.

The weirdest part happened next. I went somewhere. At first I could hear the muddled background noise of bustling nurses presumably in the room, but that disappeared and there was nothing except light. It wasn't doctor's office halogen light, it was the brightest white light I had ever seen but it didn't hurt my eyes. There were shades of blue above me and around me but this light trumped every other color and I was extremely peaceful. It was like the light exuded it's own happy medicine because I didn't even think about what had just happened. I was simply present.

In front of me was more light but it was separated into individual lights. People? Spirits? I don't know but I was in awe and felt a sense of what can only be described as reverence. They came closer but the one in the middle stood out. It was taller than the others. There was no face, nothing that would make me recognize it as a person but it felt like someone that I have known my entire life. I was THAT comfortable in their presence. I know that I was not afraid, just completely washed in a sense of…adoration. I remember kneeling down and it put its hand on me and made me feel like I was in the safest most loving place in the whole entire universe. For a moment, I didn't want to leave.

A split second later I sat up in the doctor's office so fast I almost fell off of the table and face planted onto the floor. The nurse was calmly telling me, "You are in the doctor's office, you passed out."

For a moment, in the groggy haze of my mind, I was screaming *no, no, no!* I wanted to go back to that... place. That loving awesome comfortable place. Then reality hit and I was like *what just happened?!*

I told the nurses in the room about it. I had to hear myself voice my experience to validate it. One looked at me like I had just grown two other heads. The other smiled and clapped excitedly exclaiming that she loves hearing stories from the other side. That's when it dawned on me that what I just went through was not normal. Not by a long shot. I carry that experience with me when I start to feel anxious or scared. I pass it along to clients when they need stories that bring comfort and I wrote about it here so you can see why I believe in such things!

You might have heard that children can be particularly open to the other dimensions which exist just out of our reach as well. When my oldest son was around two years old, I remember holding him while he was crying. Suddenly he perked up, started waving and smiling saying, "Hello" to someone behind me. I turned around and there was no one there. It was definitely a little disconcerting at the time!

My younger one used to lay on the floor when he was a baby, stare up into space with a huge smile and flail his arms like he was trying to grab something in mid air. I still believe they were seeing their angels. Actually, here's another story for good measure:

The kids had a video monitor in their bedrooms with a night vision camera. Every so often, like once a week? Month? I don't remember but it wasn't every day, I would wake up and check on the them by looking in the monitor on my nightstand. Let me rephrase that last thought, I would wake up and check on them every night BUT once in awhile, I'd see something in the monitor. I would look at the boys all cute and glow worm like with their zipper blanket sleepers on, when all of a sudden some of those white orbs would start floating around (like you would see on paranormal shows) which definitely look different than dust fairies. A few minutes after the floaties were darting to and fro, a white flash would cross the screen and then be gone. I always chalked it up to the spirit of the lady who passed away in our apartment before we moved in, coming to check on the babies!

Truth be told, we all have spirit guides/angels/helpers that serve as spiritual mentors since the day we are born. Some people say we have one guide that is with us throughout our lifetimes and others come in to help us work through different phases of our lives then leave when their work is finished. From what I've experienced. I believe it all to be true.

We can even call them in when we need them most. Like me for example, I have issues with anxiety and panic attacks. Whenever I know that I'm headed for a situation which could potentially launch an attack, before I go, I ask Archangel Michael to protect me and keep them from happening. Michael is considered one of the warrior types of Archangels. It helps me immensely to know that I've asked him to be there for me and have extra support from that realm. It usually seems to work but occasionally no amount of angelic help can stop my panics from happening.

I did get a pretty cool confirmation in one of my mediumship workshops when one of the students told me they saw the angel Michael with me. That was enough to give me chills as they had no idea he was my go-to angel when anxiety strikes, and knowing he's with me when I ask is just awesome!

That leads me to another piece of information when it comes to guides, angels and Archangels. Oh boy this can get confusing. I won't mention anything else about Archangels (except my Michael story) because that is certainly a whole other subject. If that interests you, I would highly recommend reading books by Doreen Virtue. She is chock full of Archangel wisdom!

Back to guides/angels. The important thing to know about them is that you need to ASK for help. From my understanding they don't often interfere unless you ask them to. There are instances when miracles happen and they seem to hop in and help without asking, or once in awhile they will give you symbolic clues to answer questions that you've been having. I'm sure there must be universal laws about that type of thing and I doubt we'll ever know how all of that stuff works. Asking also helps you to form a relationship with them to let them know, personally, that you need their help. If you feel like they've given you a message or clue without asking, you can always acknowledge them by saying, "thank you!"

You know how there are times when you can't make up your mind about something and all of a sudden out of nowhere, you feel in your heart that you know exactly what to do and it's the right decision? Or how about when you're trying really hard to figure out a problem and the answer just pops into your head out of nowhere? There are also those times when you keep seeing the same word in different places in your life, or seeing the same animals in unique ways—like you turn on the TV and see a commercial with a moose on it, and then you get in your car and drive past the Moose Lodge, and then you happen to hear the word moose in a conversation somewhere.

Those are all examples of your spirit guides trying to help you out and give you messages. It IS possible to talk to them and hear them through meditation, journal writing, dreams, or even going to a trusted medium. They are all valid ways to communicate with your guides. The best way, I feel, is to listen to your heart. Talk to your guides, intuit the answer, and know they are always there to help you on your journey.

What can they help with?

Your guide is there for you throughout your life to help you with anything and everything that you need. If you are stuck making a big decision, if someone in your life needs help, or you can't figure out which purse to buy, they can help! Well, usually. Keep in mind that they will not give you the answer, you need to figure that out for yourself, but they can give you clues to help you get where you need to be. The choices you make in life are only YOURS to make and they are well aware of this. Sometimes we just need a little confirmation that we are on the right path, and they are there to help you with that as well.

Communicate

On the next page, you'll find a few ideas to help you begin communication with your own guides, starting with meditation (surprise, surprise). Don't forget to say please and thank you. Also, have your notebook handy to write about your experience!

Who is My Guide?

1. Find your comfy spot and take a couple of deep breaths until you feel very relaxed.
2. Imagine that you are sitting in a beautiful field, full of flowers and surrounded by a forest. The air smells sweet, the temperature is perfect, you are happy and content.
3. You close your eyes to feel the sun on your face. As its warmth touches your skin, imagine that the pleasant sunshine is actually a bright white light and as it heats up your body, it is surrounding you with love and protection. You are safe here.
4. Know that you can come to this place any time that you want when you are looking for answers, need somewhere to relax, or a safe place to communicate with spirit.
5. After you feel as though you have surrounded yourself completely with the warm white sunlight, you get up to scan your surroundings. As you do this, you notice there is a path that leads into the woods. Instinctively you are aware that this path is going to lead you to your guide and without hesitation, you start to follow the trail.
6. As you enter the forest you are amazed by the amount of sunlight that is inside, almost as if the trees around you carry a light of their own. Everything in this forest has been put here by your guide to make you feel safe and secure. Every animal, every tree, everything you see contains some sort of message from your spirit guide. Take time to look around you as you continue to walk.
7. Up ahead in the distance you see a small clearing with an elegant little house. You know this house has been put here for you and that your guide is inside waiting to chat. Go to the house now and stand at the door. Pay attention to the details of the house, the door, door knob, etc.
8. Now take a relaxing, cleansing breath, set your intention that you would like to meet your guide and knock on the door.
9. If your guide does not answer then go inside of this house and explore. They may be sitting in the living room, kitchen, or another room where you would feel most comfortable.
10. When you see your guide, walk up to them and ask them their name. Ask if they have any messages for you. Spend time chatting with them. Keep in mind that your guide could appear as a person, an animal or some other unfamiliar being. They may even be invisible. See if you can feel their presence and talk to them just as if they were there. Can you feel their response? Are there no words spoken

but you are given visual cues? Use all of your senses when conversing.

11. When you feel you have spent enough time, thank them for being with you on this day and for their guidance. Close the door of the house stand in the beautiful and enchanted forest and take a deep breath.

12. Come back to the room you are in now. Take a few deep breaths, feel your feet on the floor, know that you are in the room of your home or wherever you are.

13. Write out your experience in your journal.

**

I chose the house in the woods for this meditation to give you an actual physical place where you can meet and talk to your guide. Knowing they are there and that you can come and go as you wish gives a sense of security and puts them in a realistic environment that may be easier to grasp then say, thinking they are floating all around you in your living room or something. It also is a way for you to receive symbolic messages to which I've told you about before.

Everything about the house, inside and out, and the whole environment could contain messages for you from spirit. Make sure you write everything down and try to decipher it right away or whenever you feel like doing research. Sometimes you won't even have to look things up to figure out what the messages are, you may just automatically "know". Neat, huh?

Some people that have done this type of meditation have told me cool things like a big white elephant didn't let them go into the house in the forest and they went on a journey together instead! Others have said their guides ended up being puppies, kittens, movie stars, or angels! I really did mean it when I said that sometimes you are directed to do other things. Just go with the flow and see where spirit takes you.

Also understand that it is perfectly fine if you didn't see your guide or if your guide ends up to be something that you didn't expect. Keep practicing, keep reaching out, and they will find the best way to communicate with you in the way that is right for you. Spirit is cool like that!

Other Ways To Communicate

Writing. You can set up a time to communicate with your guides through the written word. Have a pen and paper handy and set the intention that you want to talk to your spirit guide. Verbalize the fact that you only communicate with the highest and best energies. Surround yourself with white light. Ask your questions to them and start writing. Don't think about what you are writing, just start writing and see what happens. When you are done, thank your guides and read what you have written.

If you have gone off the lines of the paper, that is totally fine. If you started writing backwards, that's fine too, as long as you can read it. This is also a useful exercise for your intuition and just plain old creative writing as well. The key is to write and not think about what you are going to say next. It can be very freeing.

Talk. Simply talk to your guides out loud, whenever and where ever. Remember in the beginning of this book when I mentioned that my mom and brother busted me talking to mid air? Well, I was having a conversation with my guides. They weren't answering back, of course, I was just voicing my thoughts but my family thought I was nuts! So maybe if you do this exercise, just make sure you are alone first. Intention is everything, and thoughts are tangible. You create energy by sending it out there, voicing it instead of just thinking it is another way to set intentions.

Dreams. Before you go to sleep, while you are laying in bed, ask to meet your guides in a dream. This works great for some people and others, not so much. It doesn't work for me at all but my husband can get great messages this way. It just depends on the person and how they communicate best.

Meditating, talking, writing, and dreaming are four good ways to get the conversation started with your guides. You can do these exercises anywhere, really. If you don't feel comfortable at home, how about at church, if you attend. If you have a particular fondness for any of the symbols, angels, or idols at your place of worship, why not talk to them? Perhaps you'll get some answers that way!

If church isn't your thing then find the place that makes you feel spiritually grounded or at peace. A simple walk in the woods can open you up to animal and earth energies as well. A visit to a museum and your favorite paintings, or even making your own paintings and talking while you are creating can work as well!

It really all depends on you, your comfort level, and personal beliefs but if you want to communicate with your angels and guides, then they for sure would want to communicate right back.

Rules of the Road

It's very important to remember that when working with your guides, you should treat them as you would a close friend, always with respect, with proper manners (please and thank you) and with love in your heart.

I'm often asked if our guides have to be in the spirit world, can we have guides right here on earth. A lot of the time people are referring to their pets when they ask this. While I do not know the rules of the universe it sure does seem that certain people and animals on this earth are here just to help and guide people, doesn't it? Whether they signed some formal contract on the other side before they came here is beyond me but all I can say to that is, "probably, yes, why not?!"

The sky isn't even the limit when it comes to spirituality, there are no limitations.

LIVING WITH GRATITUDE

I have sat here for weeks (okay maybe not really sat RIGHT here for weeks because that would be silly— my kids need me and my ass would really start to hurt) but I have sat "on" this subject for awhile now. Understanding gratitude should be a very simple concept, and it really is, but writing about it in the spiritual sense proved to be harder than I thought! Honestly, I wasn't sure that I was even ready to share this topic yet but in a stream of serendipitous splendor, I was told that NOW was the time. Of course me being infamously vacuous, it took me quite awhile to realize that I was being repeatedly beat over the head with this subject.

I had put the thought out there to the universe that I wanted to explore a different topic to change the pace up a bit, something that I don't see popping off the new age bookshelves but has been equally important in my understanding of spirituality while also making me feel more grounded. I have been doing a lot of thinking in the car with the radio on in the background lately because usually the kids are quieter then, believe it or not. "Usually" doesn't mean "always" but we have our moments.

So I've been going through what I've written thus far and just couldn't quite pull out from the air what needed to come next. Around the same time of my intense pondering, I noticed that not just one but many different radio stations started to have a random resurgence of Alanis Morissette tunes. I had usually liked the songs she came out with, and not hearing them for awhile made me feel sort of nostalgic about the 90's, remembering post high-school dreams, dramas, and everything in-between. Quickly trying to squelch the little A.D.D embers that started to burn, I would remind myself to focus and think, *What should I write about next?*

One day, after what felt like the 3,000th time I heard Alanis that week it dawned on me. I felt like crowd surfing, I was so excited! About 95% of the time the song I heard was (drum roll please) "THANK YOU".

Yep. Who has two thumbs and is a wee bit airheaded... THIS GIRL! <points at self with both thumbs> Thank you universe and thank you Ms. Morissette for helping me to figure out my next chapter.

Gratitude.

I feel like gratitude is one of the most important spiritual lessons that you can learn to incorporate into your life as a parent and holistic individual yet it's highly underrated as a practice. A simple thank you can create an energy that will keep you grounded, centered, and humbled while you perform the many super duties you do throughout the day. If you don't think parenting makes you a superhero, then think back to the last time you tried to take the kids to the grocery store. There, see! You ARE a superhero!

The Gift IS the Present

Sometimes when we become wrapped up in our present situations we never have the time to really appreciate everything that we've been given. At this stage in life it seems that the only thing we can do is push forward and live in the complete now. There's not much time to dwell on the past, to dream of the future, or to have long lazy summer days to just sit and watch life unfold. Our days begin immediately (and usually way too early) with the kids needing to be fed, dressed, entertained, out the door, or any combination of those things. Career comes in between the meal preparations, music lessons or athletic practice, then it's closing the night and collapsing like you just ran a marathon only to start over again at the break of morn'. (thanks sweet Loretta Lynn for that quote! I'll be singing "Coal Miner's Daughter" the rest of the day now.)

When things get particularly tough or I get particularly tired I always stop, take a breath and say thank you. It may sound like a weird thing to do but it truly helps me to re-center and put things into perspective. Just think...in a few short years, the kids will be grown, and your days of being needed sooo much will be nothing but a fond memory. Thanking god/the universe or whoever you believe in allows you for a moment, however brief, of reflection and to put your life back into a manageable perspective. When I stop and think about this, I sort of make it sound like the whirlwind of family life is a negative thing, don't I? To that, I have to say right now that I love every darn minute of it! It's unavoidable that we have our days that we can and do get overwhelmed and exhausted and this is one of those tricks to keep you focused in times like that. Even when things are going your way a simple thank you sends out amazing energy! It does so because you are conjuring up thoughts and feelings from your heart and the very core of your soul. You essentially manifest good things to come into your life because you send good things out into the universe. At the same time saying those two little words can be extremely humbling as essentially you are giving in to the fact that there is a greater world out there that is bigger than you!

Thank You-Sizes

Expressing gratitude is probably one of the simplest meditations to perform at any time and any place but for some, it's a little hard to grasp. When expressing gratitude for something, it's not just about saying how thankful you are for your family, friends, and possessions when you go to bed at night. (Although that is a great start!) Wholehearted gratitude dives deeper than that leaving you feeling peaceful, humble, and deeply connected to your inner self and the understanding of a higher power.

A good way to start is by answering a few questions about yourself and write them down:

1. What are the things in life that make me most happy?
2. What are the things in life that I wish I could change?
3. What do I like about myself?
4. What is it about myself that I wish I could change?

Next, go over your list, visualize these things and try to feel them with your heart. Once you do that, create a statement that says something like, "I express gratitude for _____ because_____." Or a simple "Thank you for ___." is enough to start with.

When you visualize and feel each and every thing on your list, it changes your perspective— making the intangible more tangible. You may even seen details about a certain situation that you've never noticed before.

This is especially important when you are dealing with the list of things that you wish you could change. So many people I know would probably say, "I wish I had a better job, I wish I had a better education, I wish my butt wasn't so big," etc. If you look at these things individually and bring them to your heart, you'll begin to see that most of that doesn't really matter in the grand scheme of things. Gratitude is also about learning acceptance and realizing that you don't need excess to be happy. If you go through your list you may realize that you have everything you need and more!

Another way to express gratitude is to think about your body and thank it for sustaining life. Thank your lungs for processing oxygen, thank your heart for beating, thank your tummy for elimination and keeping toxins out.

How about expressing gratitude at meal time? Even if you're not the type of person who says a prayer before a meal you can still give thanks. Thanks to the farmers who harvested your veggies, the beans that give you protein, the animals, and so on.

Before the kids go to bed at night sometimes we talk about what we're thankful for. Cute and lighthearted at first, they would tell me that are thankful for pretzels and chocolate but over the months it changed. Their thank you's started to take on a different meaning as they became grateful for the grass and bugs and the ultimate heart melter from my oldest was, "I'm thankful for you, Mommy."

Can you see how working on this type of gratitude can influence change in your life? Slowly, instead of feeling so alone in the world you start to realize how connected to everything and everyone you are. It's quite humbling but very powerful at the same time.

Start by trying just once per day, to think of all the things in life you are thankful for. Incorporate the positive as well as that which you deem to be not so favorable. Even the "bad stuff" deserves attention, as it's usually the crummy things in which we learn the most lessons. Probably because they have a great impact and can stop you in your tracks to make you think about what just happened. Thank God/ Universe, etc., for throwing that fork in your path forcing you to pause and make adjustments before you move on. Try, try, try to turn self deprecating thoughts into something uplifting, concrete, and genuine.

In the case of disease, however, I would not thank anyone for giving you a disease. Unless you see the reason why it had been brought to you. I would, however, give thanks for having a body strong enough to keep fighting, thank the medicine you are taking, and so on. Empower yourself and the medicine with the healing and uplifting energy of gratitude.

As you get more comfortable try to work in a thank you whenever you deem fit, especially in times of stress, depression, or anxiety. As life sometimes seems out of control, a simple thank you can give you back a sense of control as you register to yourself and the universe that you understand things happen for a reason and you accept all that you've been given. When you do receive blessings do not forget to express gratitude for that as well! Always appreciate what you've been given and the universe will know to give you more of what makes you happiest.

Thanks to you, for reading this far!

PRAYER TACTICS

I have mentioned before that I haven't had much experience in the department of religion. Knowing that, it seems as though prayer wouldn't top the charts on my hit list of priorities. Yet prayer has always been apart of me, regardless of my background. I've always felt a deep connection to the unknown and it is that connectedness that urged me to begin having open conversations with the divine, to God, since I was a wee little lady.

These early conversations were not at all very thought provoking or profound. No... they were definitely much more simple. Here's an example that I can't believe I'm going to share but it is for the sake of a point that I immortalize it with the written word.

My parents' families lived about an hours drive from us and we used to take frequent road trips there to visit, especially over the holidays. An hour in grown up time is the equivalent to about a half century in kid world, topping that with a constant winter chill on my face as my mother had the window cracked so she could smoke cigarettes to pass the time, the car ride would last FOREVER. I was usually a pretty miserable kid on the road but I didn't complain. I looked forward to the end of her smoking sessions, the window would come up and my cheeks would be warm again. It was a pretty routine theme there in the back seat. Flick of the lighter, rumble of wind as the window is opened, icy chill on the face, smoosh sound of the finished cigarette in the ash tray, vacuum suction feeling in the ears as the window is rolled back up, blessed heat once again.

This was also before the invention of portable video games or dvd players, when we kids had to fend for our own self-entertainment. Sometimes we brought snacks. Other times my brother and I would have fights with the middle seat belt leaving one of us with some sort of bruise from being whacked with the metal buckle. Usually though, we were left alone with our thoughts, to listen to music, to wonder and daydream during the endless car ride.

I remember one particularly lengthy ride home in the cold back seat behind my mother, who was in the passenger seat. I was obsessing over something that I had seen on TV. I can't recall how old I was, definitely younger than ten though, and I was infatuated with this "new" toy that I saw someone using in an "old" movie. The toy was a pogo stick and I thought it was the most awesome thing in the whole entire world! It definitely lit up my childhood curiosity and for whatever reason, I wanted one so bad, I couldn't stop thinking about it!

I don't remember asking my parents for one but I must have and it might be possible that they said no as I felt desperate and anxious sitting there in the car all alone with my fervent thoughts about this toy. I could see my mother's dark hair peeking up over the top of the seat, my father in the driver seat and my brother next to me. As I looked around at my family, I realized that no one was paying attention to me so I clasped my hands and started praying in a disturbingly feverish manner for a pogo stick. With my head facing to my right, towards the window and tilted to the direction of the sky, I repeated my prayer continuously with eyes squeezed shut half thinking if I tried hard enough, when I opened my eyes, my cool toy would materialize itself right there on my lap.

When I finally opened my eyes, I looked forward expecting to see my mothers hair in the same place as it was before but she wasn't there! Then I saw her peaking around the side of the seat, staring at me with an awkward smile and saying with a giggle, "Jenny, what ARE you doing?"

I was so busted.

I felt stupid—but darn it I needed to be heard! I figured if my parents weren't listening then maybe God would. Embarrassed as I was, I continued on pretending that all was normal and I was just singing along to a song that was stuck in my head.

To my utter delight, a few days later on Christmas morning, Santa came through with my pogo stick! My prayers were answered! I knew I wasn't crazy even though the image of that look on my mother's face as she caught me in ridiculous prayer mode will be forever burned into my mind's eye.

It's yet another embarrassing example but I definitely have always felt that magnetism, that need to converse with the universe. Isn't that what prayer really is about? An open conversation with your understanding of the divine? To God, Goddess, Great Spirit, Buddah or whoever your go-to is—prayer is a conversation to bring you closer to them. It helps you to acquire some sort of help when it seems there is no where else to turn, to bring order and semblance to situations that may be chaotic and without end in sight.

Did you ever notice though, that usually, when you pray you are asking for something (or in my case hopelessly begging)?

"I need this, help me with that"—hopefully ending it with a "thank you."

While it's absolutely well and good to ask and receive there is another aspect of prayer I wanted to focus on. Did you know that you can use prayer as a means to keep you spiritually balanced, grounded, and centered?

As I've mentioned before and can't emphasize enough, any thought that you have creates a certain kind of energy. A positive thought creates positive energy, a negative thought creates negative energy. But a prayer can muster up some crazy big awesome energy! Why? Because usually when you pray, you do it with your whole heart and soul. A thought can flitter away from you before you even realize it, but a prayer is sort of conjured up, isn't it? You really think about what you need, you feel it reverberate so deeply, then you release it out to the universe as you speak it or say it in your head. Prayers are always answered exactly the way you NEED them to be answered. Notice I didn't say they unfold the way you WANT them to. God/the universe/your higher self knows what you need. Even if it isn't what you WANT, know that things unfold how they are supposed to—to better yourself and the life around you.

Changing your prayer tactics changes the energy, which in turn, changes the goal's outcome. The next time that you throw a prayer out there, instead of simply asking, start your prayer with a thank you.

"Thank you for letting my body deliver this healthy baby and I know this 200th night in a row of circling my home with a screaming infant will not last forever. This too shall pass. Thanks for the strength to get through this time and I look forward to the next phase, but a little help with getting us both to sleep through the night would be appreciated."

Doesn't that sound a whole lot better than, "Please god make it stop??!!!"

Can you see how changing your wording can change your intent and thus create more positive and uplifting energy? It can be humbling to give your control up to something a little higher and unseen, but knowing that your best interests are being taken care of may help balance you in the process. Most new parents (and experienced ones alike) deal with the unknowns of parenthood every day! Most of us grasp at flimsy straws trying to maintain some type of control of our busy lives, but gently breathing, changing your prayer tactics and knowing that you can gain control by creating a positive energetic environment may help you to take your power and inner strength back.

A Spoonful of Spirituality

I've already painted a pretty funny picture about how we use prayer in desperation, but what about the rest of our day? There are other ways to converse with divinity, gain balance, and send positive vibes out there when we don't really think we NEED it. This is just another way to get your dose of spiritual medicine to harmonize your energy.

In the morning. The first thing that I do in the morning (if I'm not jolted out of bed by someone screaming from a nightmare,wetting the bed, losing a stuffed animal, etc.) is say a prayer as soon as I open my eyes. I give thanks for another day of health, for the roof over our heads. A huge thanks for my beautiful family, and ask that they all be watched over as they go about their day. I ask that no harm come to them and that they continue to grow in love.

In traffic. Instead of yelling at everyone for being crazy drivers, I ask that I get to my destination safely and to allow the others on the road to breathe as they will make it to where ever they are going at some point soon. (well ok maybe 95% of the time I do that) I ask to protect all of the travelers on the road or in the air and to wrap us all in white light.

Sending the kids off to school. I ask that they are protected from bullies and that they are open to receive knowledge and are giving and helpful in the classroom and throughout their school day.

Accomplishing tasks. I ask that whatever task I need to complete, may it be completed on time, and be worthy of the effort that I put into it.

For others. Sometimes we pass a person on the street that is homeless that is crying, or looks distraught and we know there is nothing that we can do to help them. Send out a quick prayer for them for assistance with bettering their life situation, to be protected, or whatever good wish you have. If a friend is in need and you tell them that you will pray for them —really do it with your heart and soul. Visualize their situation improving. Be creative with prayer. Sometimes it's the only thing you can do when you don't know how else to help.

Hopefully the examples listed will serve as starters to get you thinking about how you can incorporate prayer to create and send good energy, bring balance, and keep a spiritual conversation going. You may begin to see for yourself spirit is always there for you to help when you need it most.

You are never alone on this earth.

THEME MUSIC FROM THE TWILIGHT ZONE

Yes it's true, we all have it. No, I'm not talking about chronic fatigue, forgetfulness or a case of the "what the heck did I just do that for's." Not like you need an example but did you ever see the movie *Look Who's Talking* where Kirstie Alley's character, Molly, was in the throws of newborn-hood when she went to prepare a middle of the night bottle for her son Mikey and ended up pouring coffee inside of the bottle instead of baby milk? That type of action is affectionately named "Mommy Brain" and we have all been there. Newborn sleep deprivation can turn even the most together type A individual into a fumbling marx brothers comedy skit. Trying to maintain balance when you are an over fatigued parent to a newborn is about as effective as writing your shopping list with a wet noodle. But I digress...

You probably can't guess by the title of this chapter whatever this "thing" is that we all possess, but I sure hope the music reference set your mind to another happy, weird, or random place. You're welcome. :)

That "thing" that we all harness within ourselves is our INTUITION and we use it more than you probably realize. Intuition can be defined and utilized in a number of different ways. It can be that one inspiring moment when you question something and your heart answers first. It is at that point (when our heart answers) where most of us start to rationalize it and change our minds only to find out we would have been right in the first place.

It can be a tool for personal growth and self realization or to help you ward off a potentially harmful situation. There are a multitude of life lessons that we have to learn and I think that a few of the toughest are to trust your own judgement, follow your instincts, and listen to your heart.

As parents we have to use our instincts all the time, don't we? Most of us can just look at our child and know deep down that something doesn't seem right with them even though they aren't verbally communicating that there might be an issue. More often than not, we are correct with our assumption!

By the time my eldest son was around three years old, we had snuggled into a pretty cozy bedtime routine. This night in particular was not much different. After dinner he had his bath, jammies were on, warm chocolate milk was in hand and *Yo Gabba Gabba* was educating him about music. After the show was over I carried him upstairs to his bed and he settled right in with his blankies, animals, and I watched as he drifted off to sleep. As I looked at his little angel face (because they instantly turn into angels when they are sleeping) I remember feeling this wave of anxiety crash against my insides but I decided to shrug it off, figuring I was overtired or something. I kissed his little forehead, went downstairs and turned his baby monitor on.

A few short hours hours later I heard him yelling for me so I checked the monitor and he wasn't there which was mega scary so I rushed over to the stairs to find him. I met his gaze as I was halfway through the short assent to his bedroom door. Before I had a chance to utter a single word I heard a loud noise which sounded a lot like,

"BLAAAAAAAARFFF!"

I apparently was standing in a very lucky spot as along with that dreadful noise, a bouillabaisse of twice eaten spaghetti and chocolate milk flew out of his tiny little frame like an angry volcano. The poor kid had the stomach flu, BAD, yet after a single sleepless night watching kid cartoons on the couch and the constant cleaning of an oversized metal bowl, he quickly recovered.

The point here is that I KNEW something was off although I suppose in this case there was really not much I could do about it but be prepared in case something wicked this way came. And it surely did!

How many times have you felt that nagging gut feeling? Did you listen to it? What happened?

In preschool we were taught that we have five senses. Nature tells us that we have SIX. Intuition being our "sixth sense." Seeing dead people isn't included in that sense. (Though it can be for some of us... would that make it seven senses?) I believe initially that our sixth sense, our intuition, was used as a survival mechanism probably to keep us on high alert from predators that would invade our spaces when we lacked doors, padlocks, and metal shuttered windows to protect us from the zombie apocalypse.

Since we have evolved from our more animalistic (for most anyway) nature to one of less hair and more sensibility (ditto), our extra sense has become more faux pas than the handle bar moustache... oh darn... hairy faces are all the rage now aren't they. How about socks with sandals? Or better yet, the always stylin', VPL! (visible panty lines in tight fitting pants). The latter keeps you staring at someone's bum for no apparent reason like you would if someone had an overwhelming pimple on their forehead or volumes of cleave pouring out of a tight, too low shirt. You really CAN'T look away no matter how hard you try. Even though all of us ladies have a set of tatas, underwear, and at least one pair of pants that are too tight… it happens. This is the human costume covering our spiritual bodies that I spoke about before. We've all been there and I am absolutely the queen of awkward moments!

Anywhoo... believe it or not, we can go back to our inner primal and use that innate sense for more than survival. We can tap that instinct and use it as a mechanism to help us grow as spiritual individuals. Working regularly with our intuition can create a continual relationship with you and your spiritual self. There is a beautiful soul that lies beneath the tight pants, bulging boobs, and socked sandal feet (that was supposed to be a joke, btw. I don't have bulging boobs and am well aware that we all look different...but for continuities sake I wrote it in there). Working with and learning to trust personal intuition helps us to learn how to have confidence with our own judgements, to encourage growth along our paths, and to tighten that bond with spirit. It gives us the freedom to make our own decisions based on what WE want, not what others think is right for us. It also helps us to teach our children how to trust their own senses when they will need these skills as they grow into adulthood. Of course, as in the case of my son's chocolate milk/spaghetti volcano incident, we can also use our intuition as a way of warning us of impending hazards that we may have to be on higher alert for.

One more reason to become best buds with your intuition is character judgement. Sometimes you meet someone and get a dodgy feeling from them right away, other times you instantly adore someone. Trusting your gut could save you a heap of trouble in many different situations like finding babysitters, job interviews, staying at hotels, potential dates and many other situations—social or otherwise.

Not too long ago a mentor of mine, Pastor Robin, said something in class that really struck home. She said that one mustn't "should" themselves. (The first time she said it in class, I seriously thought she said not to SH$T yourself. No kidding. I stared in astonishment for a couple of minutes until it sunk in what she actually said. Looking around the room I noticed that I wasn't the only one a little confused.) Do you know what "shoulding" yourself means? Think about all the small conversations that you have with yourself every day. I should do this or I should do that. You do things based on what others expectations are of you ALL the time. You say I really want to go skiing this weekend but I "should" catch up on housework instead. Dudette, go skiing. Housework can wait. Chip at it during the week or just don't invite anyone over until spring. If you skipped skiing you not only missed a day of killer exercise and an excuse to have a Bloody Mary or hot tea at the lodge, you could have had some other opportunity open up for you when you went.

When you "should," you close your door on a new path. Your intuition tells you to go and do it but you knock it down when you make excuses. Dare to do what you dream, even if it's just the dream of the moment like a wicked ice cream craving in the middle of winter. Go do it and see what happens. Listen to your intuition as long as it is for your best and highest good.

After reading all this happy fluffy stuff about why intuition usage is a good thing, why is it that we no longer believe in or use this sense to its fullest? Don't you think it needs to be utilized in our every day life just like our vision, hearing or taste? I sure do!

When you're flying solo on this spiritual journey, especially while juggling babies and the rest of your life, it can be difficult to incorporate yet another mental post it note to blow off your desk when someone walks by. Believe me, I know how hard it is to start a new and good habit. I don't even bother to make New Year's resolutions anymore because I never keep them, heck, I rarely even make it past the first day!

With this in mind, in the following pages I've included some seeds to help you begin working with and honoring your intuition—to help you plant another flower in your spiritual garden.

Meditation for Opening Your Intuition

It figures that meditation would be the first tool on my list even though it usually is the most difficult for everybody, myself included! I just adore the practice and even though it's hard to squeak it in sometimes, it really is worth it. One sneaky way to zen for a few minutes is in the middle of the night. Try meditating yourself to sleep after a bathroom visit. During the day you can lock yourself in the closet for three minutes, meditate IN the bathroom, or you can always use the I'm going to lay on the floor with my eyes closed for five minutes while the kids jump on me meditation. (It's worked for me on many occasions!) Any amount of time quieting your mind is so useful and rewarding. Let's face it, being a parent and having to be constantly one minute ahead of your kids works a number on your brain. At the end of the day I feel like I'm ready for a cocktail and usually it's just to compliment the pile of mush that my brain already is.

So without further ado, here is a quick and effective meditation for you to try. Read through it first so you don't have to keep opening your eyes to find out what to do next, unless you need or want to. Don't worry about the exact visual steps, it's really up to you to go where your mind wants to take you. Likewise, don't forget that you can record the steps on your smartphone and play it back. It works but I don't usually do it because I shutter when I hear my own voice. Silly, but true.

Before you begin, think of a question or something in your life that you really need an answer to. If there's nothing pressing and when it's time to ask, simply state, "What do I need to know in my life right now for my best and highest good?"

Keep your journal handy to write down your experience and any symbols received!

Give the following meditation a whirlski and see what happens.

The Gift

1. Close your eyes and take a couple of deep breaths.
2. Know that you are safe and entering a place of total protection for you to explore your intuition in peace and solitude.
3. Imagine now that you are standing on a well worn path of dirt and grass in the middle of a beautiful forest.
4. Look around you. What do you see? What color are the trees? Are there animals?
5. Look above you. Notice how blue and beautiful the sky is. Are their birds flying overhead?
6. Take another deep breath and fill your lungs with the beauty that surrounds you. Can you smell the pine, the mulch below your feet, the clean forest air?
7. Walk along your path, feel the earth below your feet and notice how grounded you feel as you walk.
8. Take another deep breath and relax feeling blissful and free as you walk.
9. You hear the sound of running water in the distance, and follow the path towards the sound as it has sparked your curiosity.
10. The sound grows louder as you walk until you see a running stream just ahead. Notice the details. How big is it? How fast is the water running?
11. As you approach the bank of this stream you feel somehow that it was put here just for you to admire its beauty and to remind you that you have a special connection to the earth and to the divine.
12. With this realization, your heart opens and you feel incredibly alive and at peace.
13. You happen to look at the ground now and realize that before you is a box with a lid.
14. Take note of the box. What does it look like? Is it simple like a shoe box? Is it an ornate metal box covered in jewels? An old wooden treasure chest?
15. Whatever it looks like, know that it was put here for a reason and is constructed to your likeness, and speaks to you in ways that only YOU would understand. Inside this box lies the answers to all of your questions and you just have to believe in yourself, in your faith, that the answers are this close to you.
16. Now state your question. Feel the question from the very depths of your core. Remember if you can't think of one, simply say "What do I

need to know in my life right now to benefit my highest and best good?"
17. Now it's time to open the box and see what is inside of it. (The key here is not to try too hard to search for an answer, just relax, keep an open mind, and see what happens!)
18. Close the box, take a deep breath, and come back to the room you were in.
19. *Make sure to say thank you for the gifts you received. You're not only showing gratitude to spirit or the divine, or whoever you believe in, you are also giving yourself respect. Saying thank you in this regard is a reminder that you do have the power within you to find the answers and create change when needed.

***

Okay, I know that seems rather long, but I assure you it really isn't. Once you get the hang of this meditation you can scale it down to fit your needs. The point is to really try and be still for a few minutes, totally engorge all of your senses, and trust your intuition!

If you do choose to skip a couple of steps because of time restraints or whatever please never forget the following:

1. Deep breaths.
2. Feeling your feet on the ground.
3. Total relaxation (no anxiety in your happy place)
4. Trust.
5. Gratitude.

Please also record everything that you can remember in your journal. If you can't right away, then do a voice memo on your phone or tape recorder and write it in later. Journaling is so relevant when tracking your progress.

On a final note, don't worry if there was nothing in your box at this time. You could have been trying too hard, you could need more practice, or maybe you already know the answer to your question! :)

Learning to trust yourself is the main goal of the meditation. Just keep trying and use this little exercise to help you gain faith in the deepest parts of you as a spiritual being.

Divining Your Way

It's definitely not a secret that aside from meditation and Reiki, I'm an enormous fan of the Tarot. If the thought of tarot gives you the shivers because it reminds you of childhood images of dingy storefronts baring creepy neon "psychic" signs blinking and making noises like a bug zapper, harboring a crazy-haired woman pointing at you with a crooked finger beckoning you inside, then fear no more. I'm certainly not scary (though my kids may beg to differ when I give them the "I'm not pleased" face) and neither are the many amazing tarot practitioners that I've met in my lifetime. I'm here to tell you that this is not the work of fire and brimstone. Tarot cards, like meditation, are a just a tool to help you open up and trust your intuition. That's it! So if you feel like reading along with one eye open then I'll be here with my DIY painted finger-nailed hand to hold yours the whole way. Promise!

Just so you know, I'm not going to give you lessons on how to read for other people at this time (though.. hmmm...maybe that would be in my cards for the future) I'm going to show you how the Tarot can be another method of forming a bond of trust within yourself. It will be hard at first to be completely non judgmental of the answers that you receive especially if the answers that you get are positive. It's definitely harder to believe the good stuff. We humans are such gluttons for punishment, aren't we?

Instinctively, most people would probably want to shush the happy news away and put the deck back in their nightstand drawers because these things are "not working" or the answers are being "made up." I can tell you first hand that more times than not you will find out that you are right! Deep breathing, letting go of expectations, your ego, and trusting yourself will keep you on the right track with this tool.

If you do decide to buy a deck and try it out, have fun in the process! There are thousands of beautiful tarot decks to choose from. Just make sure you buy two of the same. If the kids get a hold of them, your deck will be history. Trust me. The kids love to play cards and I'm still missing my favorite ones at the moment. Sigh.

When you are out there perusing the virtual or real store shelves for a tarot deck to work with, you will probably come across other "oracle" types of cards and tools as well. There are Rune cards and stones, Angel Message Decks, Animal Totem cards, and a plethora of others to choose from. I would recommend starting with a deck of cards that specifically says "Tarot" and then if you find you are drawn to other types of cards by all means buy whatever you want. Tarot to me is sort of like learning the notes before you play in a band. It's a fabulous introductory tool. If you feel drawn to use some other oracle cards first, however, then go for it! Just maybe stick to one thing at a time for awhile so you don't confuse yourself. All the different ways to read cards and their definitions can get overwhelming.

Tarot to Go

I took a Tarot class once. It was short, just a few weeks long, but still chalk full of history and good information. None of which I remember. Actually when I think really hard there are only a few select things that I can recall which I'll happily share with you right now:

1. The devil card does NOT mean satan or evil. It usually represents a person with an addiction or the shadow side of yourself.
2. The death card does NOT mean you are going to die. You will never get a reading that time stamps your terminal departure. EVER. If you ever come across a tarot reader that does this or wants to charge you to remove some sort of crazy spell that was cursed upon you then do me a favor—RUN don't walk to the nearest exit and get out. Those people just play on vulnerability and want your hard earned duckets. Find someone you can trust. Word of mouth is usually best in my opinion. The death card actually represents change. A change that is coming or a change that just took place. It also means the end of a situation and the inevitable start of something new. No dying allowed here!
3. There is a card that some of us tarot readers affectionately dub the "Oh SH-T" card. It's called the Tower and represents some sort of upheaval going on around you.
4. The Queen of Swords is the Mommy Card. In other words, it represents a maternal influence.

Lessons 1-4 are all about individual cards. I don't know why I chose to remember those but for whatever reason, they stuck with me. I suppose it would make sense for two of the three for me to remember, but who knows about the Queen?

5. This final lesson is what REALLY helped me grow confidence and begin trusting my intuition more soundly. Ready for this? Each deck comes with a little "how to" guidebook. Even though there are a huge variety in the style of cards, their definitions and the way certain symbols are laid out in the pictures are relatively the same. Each book will have slight variations but they are all pretty similar, otherwise. When you open

the deck and take that little book out, I was taught to chuck the book in the trash. Yep...THROW IT AWAY!

GASP! But how will I know what the cards mean, you ask? You don't! And that's the point of intuitive tarot. You let your intuition guide you, let your spirit tell the story, not the words on the paper. For study purposes though I would suggest keeping the book around. It's interesting to learn the true meanings and sometimes can even help you intuitively as you are pondering over an answer, but I wouldn't rely on them forever as it is always best to use your own judgement, which comes directly from your heart. Overtime, you'll be able to tell the difference between the info you are feeding yourself and what truly comes from the inside.

I'm going to skip ahead here and assume you have a tarot deck in your hand right now. Truth be told, you can also do this with a deck of playing cards but the visual cues from a beautifully crafted tarot deck can set your ethereal mind a-soaring so I think it best to start there. Ultimately though, it's up to you.

I know you'll want to tear open the box and get playing right away which is fine and dandy but make sure after that you take care to keep them with you and allow them to become apart of your energy. With energy I just mean I want you to feel sooooo super comfortable with them in your hands. I want you to make them YOURS. I'm thinking more like an old blown out pair of jeans that you just can't part with. There are dozens of ways to do this but the simplest thing I suggest is to carry them around with you if possible, in your purse, diaper bag, car, or wherever they can be close to you.

When you get an extra minute just leaf through them and study their images. See how you react to each card, mentally, emotionally, even physically. When you put them away, use something that will keep them all together in one safe place. Typically you would put them in something dark like a cloth bag or wooden box. Dark is good so the sunlight doesn't fade the pictures. Some people buy ornate boxes or bags to carry them around. ANYTHING will do. A lot of decks come with their own little pouches now. I think the first homemade pouch I had for my cards was the purple cloth bag a bottle of Crown Royal Whiskey came in. Thanks Dad! :)

Finally, store them close to you at night. Put them on your nightstand, under your pillow, under the couch cushion, where ever you will be close to them while you're sleeping. At night, our aura's and spirits are the most open as our minds relax from outside influences. It's good to keep the cards nearby to sort of impart your energy onto them. Basically you want to get them used to you and you to them, like...a pet made out of thick card stock...I guess...okay, I'm losing it. Moving on....

Some people also like to "cleanse" their decks to get rid of any other energy that may have been attached to them at the factory or from previous owners if the deck is a used one. Remember the world of energy I mentioned awhile back—how thoughts are things and how you have the power to shape your life based on your very own happy way of thinking? Everyone has their own unique energy and you leave bits and pieces of that energy where ever you go. Sort of like your own personal stamp of approval branded on an object or a place. It's how you can pick up a piece of fruit at the grocery store and put it back because it doesn't seem right but are ok with a nearly identical piece of fruit sitting next to it. It probably had an energy that didn't mesh well with yours from the person that picked it up prior to you!

Cleansing Ideas:

1. **Smoke on the Water.** Use smoke from incense or a smudge stick (A bundle of herbs like sage, lavender, mugwort, sweetgrass, or others that you can find at most new age stores) Light one end, blow it out, and pass the cards through the smoke that follows. This is a very popular form of cleansing that is effective for more than just cards! We all interact with many different types of people every day. Sometimes these interactions can leave you drained or feeling a little off because you pick up people's energy and they stick to your aura. By smudging (using the smoke from a smudge stick to cleanse) you can clarify the air of unwanted energies that surround yourself, your belongings, your kids, your house! Just be careful because those things can get SUPER smokey and always carry a fireproof container with sand or salt on the bottom to catch any hot embers that may fall. Of course if there are allergies or asthma then this definitely wouldn't be an option.

2. **Werewolves of London.** Use the energy of the moon! Keep your cards on a windowsill to soak in the moonlight (during a full moon is especially beneficial).

3. **Earth Angel.** Place your cards in a bowl of soil to let the earth soak up the energy.

4. **Crystal Blue Persuasion.** Surround your cards with cleansing crystals such as hematite or clear quartz. You could even put smaller crystals directly in your carrying bag or case and keep them always with your cards. Just remember to cleanse the crystals once in awhile using any of the ideas from this list.

5. **Salt of the Earth.** Sea salt is your friend. People have been using sea salt as a means of cleaning negative energies for a long, long, long time! Place your cards in a bowl of sea salt to keep them clean and pure. You can even put some salt in the bag or box that you put your cards in.

As you can see there are lots of different ways to clear the cards (and other things) of unwanted energy. Do you HAVE to cleanse the cards like this? No, you don't. Some people will tell you it's vital and necessary but I believe that if it doesn't make you comfortable at first then don't do it. I do encourage you to give it a try at some point just to see if you can feel or notice a difference in the cards themselves or with your own practice with self-reading. Using your other senses, your "feeling" or "clairsentience," is ANOTHER way of developing and trusting your intuition! If you are comfortable with trying one of the cleansing techniques just for experimental purposes then by all means, go for it! Slowly though, I would ask that you try to incorporate some sort of purification practice that you are comfortable with for your tools and even yourself at the end of the day.

SPREAD EM'!

A spread is what it's called when you lay the cards in front of you and get ready to read them. There are as many different layouts or spreads as there are tarot cards and one is not better than the other. The book your cards came with probably has examples too so feel free to experiment, experiment, experiment! You can even come up with your own spread, it won't make the answers wrong and honestly it's probably best to personalize as it's imparting your own energy and wisdom into the deck. For time and ease though, we're going to work with a simple three card spread.

1, 2, 3, Help Me!
1. Start with a question that you need help with.
2. State your intention that you wish to find the answers that will honor your greatest and highest good. (or some other uplifting blessing for your reading)
3. Hold your cards, take a couple of deep breaths, keep the intention that you need answers for your greater, highest and best good, and state your question.
4. Lightly shuffle the cards.
5. Take three cards from the top of the deck and lay them out in a row in front of you. Alternately, you can spread the cards out in front of you face down and choose any three that you are drawn to.

Totally off the subject but since I've been writing this chapter I keep singing "The Gambler" by Kenny Rogers. "You gotta know when to hold em..." Anyway, you have the cards in front of you now. What comes next?

You can think of the cards in one of two ways. Traditionally you would look at them from left to right. Card 1 would represent the history of the situation or the "Past". Card 2 is the "present" highlighting what is currently going on and Card 3 would be the "Future" or the outcome.

While many many people read them this way, I have to admit that I'm too impatient. I understand that sometimes it's good to know the past of the situation because it will help you fully understand how you got to this point in your life but most of the time I know how I arrived at the current predicament and don't care to relive how it all came into place. Therefore, I like to see the cards a little differently.

I use the middle card, the number two card as the indicator of the predicament. Then I look at the left card (#1) and the right card (#3) to tell the story. In either case you can read them like this:

Look at each card thoroughly. Study the images, think of the names that are on the cards. Do any of the images or words stick out to you for any particular reason? Is there anything you are drawn to? Keep looking, meditate on them, relax and don't think too hard! When you over think then your intuition shuts down and you are left staring blankly not unlike the look your kids give you when you ask them to do anything that requires effort, like clean their rooms.

Look again at the pictures on all of the cards and allow them to tell you a story. For example, sometimes you see that the people or animal figures are facing each other. Other times you will find that they are looking away from each other. Those two examples alone contain some pretty interesting symbolism. If they are looking towards one another it might be a hint that "things are coming together." If they face away, it could mean that things aren't quite being seen "eye to eye". Do you understand what I'm saying? Look closely and see if the cards are telling you a story.

You can always lay out one more card from the top of the pile if you need further clarification. Suppose you laid out "the sun" card. That, to me, would predict a favorable outcome. If you got something like the Tower though, don't freak because it doesn't mean anything terrible. Definitely don't worry about that if it happens! The same qualifies if you pulled out the devil or death card for that matter. Again, those typically symbolize some sort of inevitable change coming... not disaster or damnation.

Write down in your journal anything that you are drawn to. Then think about what those symbols could mean to you personally, afterwards. You can definitely look in the information book that came with your deck for clues if you want or you can search online for the meaning of certain symbols as well. I find it best to go with your own instincts and interpretations though because every symbol is personal to only you! The idea here is not to doubt but to trust that you have the ability to figure it out on your own.

To recap what I just said:
1. Look at the cards and take note of what pictures or words stand out to you. Does any card or image invoke a certain feeling for you?
2. Don't worry if you get one of the "scary" cards that ARE NOT scary at all. They usually symbolize some sort of change— or to take it a step further, sometimes they ask you to look at your own "dark side" or part of you that you are holding on to and probably need to let go of.

3. Write it all down so you can remember to look it up later or use your own intuition to interpret the meaning.

Once you relax and let go of your expectations, other senses may start to kick in as well. Flashes of information might pop into your mind —like the pictures you see in your head when you are trying to remember something, except you weren't doing anything but looking at the cards. You might hear in your head a word or phrase, you may even get a strong feeling or a "knowing" about something. Hey, don't look at this page like its crazy, this stuff happens! It's all apart of opening up to your higher self and to spirit in whatever form that may be to you.

When you are finished, express gratitude in your own way for any information you were able to obtain about your situation. Mom taught us to say please and thank you, we hound our kids to say thank you and that same rule applies here too! Respect your divinity, respect the process, respect yourself. Thank you!

Lastly, ground and close. Put your hands on the ground, wipe your hands like you are getting invisible dirt off of them, wash your hands, anything that breaks the energy of what you were doing to bring you back to the here and now. Better yet, let the kids back into the room! But don't let them in before you "close". By "closing" you simply state out loud or in your mind, that you are ending this session with love or anything that is positive, uplifting, and says that you are done! As always, write down what happened during your session.

Does this sound scary to you still or do you see how the cards are really just a catalyst for you to ignore outside influences and connect with your personal divinity and intuition?

Remember to cleanse, ground yourself, look, relax, listen and trust yourself! Also write down any impressions you get so you can go back later and see how much you've grown!

Last but certainly not least... how on earth can you do all this with the kids around? Well if they're bitty babies that's pretty easy. They can lay on the floor with you while you're messing with the cards, or they can kick around in the bouncer or hangout on your lap. Wherever really. Toddlers are more difficult but maybe a few minutes of playing during their nap time would be sufficient. Be creative. Incorporate the older kids if you want. Or hide in your closet. :) Where there's a will, there's a way!

The Others

Here is a short list of other tools you can use to approach your personal intuitive development. It's definitely not comprehensive as there are zillions of things out there for you to play with and I certainly don't have enough energy to create the ultimate list. Besides that, I'd rather stick to the ones I've tried and experienced. If you are feeling saucy you can do research on your own time and see if these speak to you on any level.

*Don't forget: Cleanse, Set Happy Intentions, Show Gratitude, Ground, and Close.

Pendulums. Fun and freaky all at the same time

A pendulum is simply a weight that is suspended by some sort of string, rope, or chain. Think: The swinging action of a grandfather clock.

How many of you tried the trick where you stick a wedding ring or needle on a thread and let it circle around your belly to find out the sex of the baby? That's a pendulum!

I seriously have no idea how it works but it really seems to, though I do know a few people who can't get the darn thing to move no matter what. Pendulum's are amazing tools for a number of things like pointing in certain directions to help you find lost items or answering yes or no questions.

You can buy beautiful handmade pendulums at specialty gem stores, new age, or even some book stores but you don't need to go all out to experiment. Put a piece of jewelry on a necklace—like Carrie from *Sex and the City*. She never wore her engagement ring on her finger, right? That makes a perfect pendulum.

Swingers:
1. Hold the pendulum between your first couple of fingers with your dominant hand so that the weight hangs freely.
2. Place your other hand palm up below the hanging pendulum.
3. Now go ahead and ask the pendulum to swing in a way that you will recognize as yes.
4. Don't have a cow when the pendulum starts swinging by itself.
5. Don't have twin cows when you ask it to swing faster and it does.
6. Next, ask it to swing in a way that you will recognize as "no."
7. Now that you've established yes and no go ahead and ask your questions!
8. Do it with a friend! No not THAT. Shame on you! Ask questions only your friend knows the answer to and see how the pendulum fairs.
9. The kids would have fun playing with this one as well if they're old enough to understand. Otherwise the baby might eat your wedding ring or stuff it somewhere bizarre like in their diaper or something. Maybe it would be best to keep this to yourself, after all.

Scrying Game

Picture this, will you? It's a sunny day with lazy, light puffy clouds floating by. The weather is perfect, the breeze is warm and you are laying on the grass basking in the sunshine, looking up at the sky. Not having much time to do this as an adult, until recently when my babies became old enough to do this with me, I think back to how magical it felt (and is now again) when I was little to be carefree, let my mind go, and see the clouds transform and tell their stories. These days we talk about how this cloud looks like a dog or dinosaur, and that one looks like a toilet or the Titanic. It's sort of a right of passage for kids, I think. They are "allowed" to dream with their eyes open and by "allow" I mean that they allow themselves because they aren't bound by the same stuff that we so called grown ups bind ourselves up with. (fear, regret, conformity, responsibility, etc.) What most people don't realize, is that cloud gazing is pretty much a form of scrying.

The dictionary says that scrying means, "to divine, especially by crystal gazing." The thought of "crystal gazing" reminds you of witches and crystal balls doesn't it? Well there are even more ways to scry besides using a crystal ball. Remember the Disney movie, *Snow White*? Think: Dark mirror. Incantation spoken, "Mirror, mirror on the wall...," then a spirit appears to tell the witch whatever she wants?

You guessed it. You can scry with a dark mirror too! Oh joy! The media has made scrying a super creepy practice but the real purpose goes beyond that and just like tarot, it isn't scary. If you're more of a realist and are thrown off by the idea of scrying then take note, it's not just about the woo woo world or good television. By gazing into a dark mirror, you are looking into a "mirror" but you don't really see the physical you. Perhaps you see a shadow of yourself, or nothing at al. This simple act allows you to gets rid of the "ego-self" to let your inner you shine through!

You can use scrying as a tool to help you unlock your subconscious mind—the inner part of yourself that has the answers but your rational mind is too busy thinking to listen to it. If you learn to trust yourself and the information you receive, you can benefit from this practice as a way of developing your intuition, concentration, trust and confidence. Plus it's fun!

What tool do you use?
Whatever feels right to you! Here's a short list of ideas. You can be creative as well.

Crystal ball
Scrying mirror (glossy black mirror)
Candle flame (just don't look directly into the flame, gaze above or below)
Fireplace or campfire
Bowl of water with a few ink drops placed inside
Dark bowl of water with candles placed on either side
Tea leaves
The clouds
Your creativity

How do I start?
Make sure you have your notebook handy to write about your experience.

Before you begin it's important to set a positive intention. Say something like, "I'm doing this with the intention of pure love and light." You may also want to burn sage or spread around sea salt to get rid of any unwanted energies that are hanging around and to put you in the mood. Music helps too!

Now what?
You've chosen your tool, cleared the air, and set your intention. Next comes your question. But what should you ask? Your question could be about a past or future event or a general one like, "What do I need to know in my life right now?" You could even ask about a past life if you feel so moved. Just make sure your intention is positive and you're coming from a place of love.

Now start your gazing!

1. You want to be very relaxed.
2. Soften your eyes, let them lose their focus.
3. Just gaze and drift.
4. Try not to think about anything and stay in the moment. And don't try too hard! If you force it, nothing will happen besides a headache, trust me on this one.

What are you supposed to be seeing?

The reason why most people give up is because they have no idea what they're looking for. The general expectation is for the whole room to disappear and a magical flatty TV screen will appear while your answer is vividly displayed in sharp images and surround sound audio. While that would be awesome, it's soooo not how it works.

First impressions are everything. And remember not to dismiss ANYTHING. Write out whatever comes to you. Pay attention to the way you are feeling. Your mood. Your body temperature. Did your mood change? Did your environment change somehow? Is the air heavier or lighter?

Is your imagination suddenly activated and you find yourself thinking or dreaming of other things? Do you see flashes of images or symbols—especially ones that don't make any sense? The most abstract visuals are usually the ones that have the most meaning!

Don't forget that when working with any sort of divination, the answers are usually extremely symbolic. Just as with the Tarot cards, sometimes it helps to search the internet for what the symbolism may mean. The most important thing, however, is for you to consider the symbol or image yourself and figure out what it represents to you. This is also why it's important to write everything down, so you can go back later and decipher the code.

When you're all done, it's always nice to show your gratitude for any messages received. (As you know, gratitude is a great practice to help your spiritual growth anyway, so why not start here?) State with a positive intention that you're done by saying something along the lines of, "I end this session with white light and love." Or whatever works best for you.

Scrying is a very fun practice that helps you learn how to open and trust your intuition. Don't fret if it doesn't "work" for you. It may click one day or it may not. Also keep in mind that some people just don't receive information visually, they use other senses such as feeling, hearing, taste or smell!

Keep trying if you like or move on and do something else. Remember to not dismiss any impression that you may get from your scrying sessions and most of all, enjoy the process!

Guess Who?

The final tool I'm bringing up to help you build (and trust) your intuitive skills isn't so much of a tool as it is a game. Exciting, yes? I'm sure you'll have fun doing this but don't let it discourage you. I've messed with this many times and I'm still really bad at it! Not that how I operate means anything at all, but just saying, even with lots of practice I have never gotten better. Knowing that, you may do awesome at this or you may not but it will be fun trying. Have the kids play too!

This game kind of reminds me of that scene in *Ghost Busters* where Peter Venkmen (Bill Murray) was testing the ESP abilities of two people. He sits across from his subjects, a male and a female, both of which are hooked up to electrodes. He holds in front of him a large playing card that faces him so only he knows if there is a square, triangle, squiggly lines, or another shape on it. The two people have to guess what's on the card that Peter is holding and if they are wrong, they will get an electric shock. Of course the one participant is a swanky blonde and the other is a man that holds no interest for Peter. You can guess what happens next. The poor guy gets all the shocks while the blonde is miraculously and amazingly psychic as she "guesses" every card perfectly. Yes, Peter lied about her "abilities" to score a date.

In my guessing game, not only can I promise you some fun, but I guarantee that you won't get an electric shock, and I won't ask you out on a date. Instead, I'll ask that you get a set of regular playing cards, or buy white card stock/thick pieces of paper where ink on one side won't bleed through to the other. If you go the card stock route here's what you can do with them:

1. Cut the stock paper into ten equal squares.
2. Pick five shapes you'd like to work with.
3. Draw one shape on one side of a card.
4. Draw another shape on one side of a different card and so on until you have five cards each with a different shape on one side of them.
5. Do this again with the same shapes on the last five cards leaving you with a set of ten cards with shapes on one side.
6. If you prefer color over shapes, use crayons or whatever you have and color a little bit on one side. One color per card, making sure you cannot see the color on the other side.

7. To make it even more adventurous, try drawing the shapes in different colors. Be daring! :)

Playing The Game
1. Shuffle the cards.
2. Pick one up and make sure that you don't see what's on the other side.
3. Take a deep breath, relax, and release your mind.
4. Think to yourself, *what shape/color/is on the other side of this card?*
5. Wait and see if something comes to you.
6. Don't try too hard, just relax and let go.
7. Write down any first impressions. You could have a feeling about it, see a color, hear something, have a random image in your head. Whatever it is, stop right there and write it down.
8. Turn the card over and see if it matches the impression that you received.

This is an excellent tool for trusting and developing intuition as well as deciphering symbolism. For instance, if a red Volkswagen Beetle popped into your head during the exercise it could be referring to a color or shape that was on the card (or even the card after that one).

The "beetle" aspect could be a symbolic message to you, too! (think totem/spirit animal/musician) It's not uncommon for you to receive messages while you are practicing these exorcises as you are opening yourself up to a higher frequency.

If you decided to try this with a deck of playing cards, guess which color, suit, or number is next before you flip the card over.

Always record your results and ground yourself.

Another variation of the guessing game can be played sans cards with a friend or the kids. Think of a color and ask the other person what color you were just thinking of. (I do this with my boys all the time. It's an awesome distraction when they're about to melt down over something.) The trick is to really see the color in your mind and hold it there while the other person/people are thinking.

Next, try the same thing and then hold the other person's hand before they guess. Does one way work better than the other? You may find that you can pick up more energy with gentle touch than without physical contact. Experiment and see how you do!

See! Told you it was fun!

Babies and kids learn how their environment and world works through the power of play. Even though we are adults, we are no exception to this rule. Through "playing" with these different extra sensory developmental tools we learn how our own intuition works and how to access it when we need an answer or a gentle nudge from spirit that we are on the right path.

It's important to note, however, that when we step out of these boundaries and try our hands at using these tools to read for other people, we are entering into a whole other world of responsibility. That is why I do not advise you to try and read for other people whatsoever. At least not through the use of this book. This book and chapter is for your own self discovery and personal growth.

Since you are only using these tools for personal growth, please know that sometimes we have days when we just shouldn't be playing and need to focus on grounding instead. I've never had this happen, personally, but if for whatever reason, your own interpretations lead you to a result that appears "negative," I ask that you close what you are doing and give yourself time to ground and balance. You will never get an answer that isn't supportive to your greater good and you must make sure that your mind, body, and spirit are in balance before you can play.

If you are in good spirits (no pun intended) then break out the goods, play and learn as if you are an eager child discovering a whole new world.

Sometimes when you open yourself up to higher frequencies as you do when using your intuition and practicing with tools like scrying and Tarot cards, your body needs time to adjust. You may find yourself a little more tired than usual or getting small headaches. It doesn't always happen but I have witnessed it in some people. If this is the case with you, please ALWAYS make sure that you ground yourself and close your practice session using the methods I've mentioned previously or creating a gentle and safe method that works for you. Doing so will bring your energy back into balance. Also, reducing the frequency in which you use your tools will help as well. Sometimes it's better to slowly integrate a new practice and let your body and mind get used to it. Just like any new hobby, project, or area of study, too much too fast can make your body want to put on the brakes to absorb the information.

Always remember to take a deep breath, set good intentions, ground, close, and be ready to open the door for new opportunities to learn and develop!

CYCLES

Growing up, I never really saw myself as wanting to be a mother. I wanted to be an actress, a teacher, a writer, to acquire some sort of odd job in the music business as well as other career choices I'm sure, but being a mom never charted on my list of things "to be."

It wasn't until my early twenties when something inside of me clicked and made me realize that I wanted and needed family of my own more than anything. Part of the reason, I believe, was to replace the one that had sort of fallen apart when my mother passed away and the other part of me just wanted a really good excuse to watch Saturday morning cartoons again. Little did I know that those Saturday morning cartoons were replaced by like three television channels with 24 hours of very bizarre animated cartoonish type of thingies. Boy did I have a lot to learn! That was sarcasm, by the way. There were definitely more reasons than cartoons for me wanting to become a mother, I assure you. :)

I ended up having my first child at 29 years old, and up until that point I could probably count on one hand how many times I've ever babysat in my entire life. I knew nothing and I mean NOTHING about babies except for what I've seen on TV, which we've all discovered is devoid of any semblance of reality.

When the doctor handed me my beautiful son I thought that I would have no problem figuring out how to work this little miraculous wonder...until I tried to breastfeed. That was my first hiccup. How could something so holistic, natural and beautiful turn into a sweaty, heart palpitating and stressful mess? Just trying to get the kid to "latch" on was like a three hour nightmare! Finally when the boob nazi (to which I affectionately called the militant hospital lactation consultant) came in the room I felt a sense of relief—until she said to cup my boob like a sandwich.

Oookaaaay? Like a whole wheat sandwich or a Hoagie? What the heck are you talking about, lady?

Yeah, so needless to say when she left my hospital room I was more confused than when she came in. I succeeded here and there but it wasn't until the day we came home that I managed to rock the breastfeeding. Desperation to deflate the cantaloupes that had appeared on my chest where the b-cups formally took residence, we called another lactation consultant to pay me a visit. When Super Boob Woman left that glorious first day, I was 1,0000% more confident about my breastfeeding skills, which naturally spilled over into baby rearing self-confidence. I knew I could totally handle this baby thing and felt it with all of my proud mommy heart. After the door closed behind my new favorite lady, I looked lovingly at my son who was now latched onto me feeding like a champ, only to discover that I had put my poor baby's diaper on backwards. It was the middle of July and that was all he was dressed in that particular day. Super Boob Woman must have thought I was out of my mind. Yes, yes I had it all figured out.

Not!

When my second son came along and the baby to parent ratio in the house during the day was 2:1 I became very overwhelmed and depressed. I think when you're in the middle of something, sometimes the only perspective you can see is what is right in front of you. At this point in the baby game, I thought for the rest of my life I would be puked on, pooped on, screamed at, sleep deprived, and I had no where to turn. I had no friends with kids, no family around, and my husband worked very long hours and traveled a bunch. I was stuck hovering above Manhattan all alone with tiny people who demanded my every last morsel of attention... it was hard, but believe it or not I have fond memories of our time together in our little brick nest in the sky.

As life would have it, they actually do grow from infants to toddlers, to kids, (who knew?!) and things became easier in a sense (only to be replaced with big kid problems) but still easier as they communicate much better as they get older.

One day as I was looking back at those early days of motherhood, I happened to remember something my mother in-law said once which really put things into perspective for me and probably would have helped to lift me out of that early funk a lot sooner had I remembered it. She said "This too shall pass." Boy was she right, it sure did pass more quickly than I had ever imagined and before I knew it, we were onto the next phase of our lives. I realized then, well I always knew really but it all sort of made sense at this point, is that we, every single one of us, and life itself exists on a series of cycles.

If you think about it simply, there is no up without a down, no left without a right, top without a bottom, in without an out, light without dark, etc. Just about every aspect of life exists within a circle or phase. Paying particular attention to your babies and kids will give you first hand witness to the beginning and end of phases. (Think terrible two's and three's. Oye!)

Who knows this cyclical routine more than mother nature herself? Just look at the change of seasons, if you are fortunate enough to live in a part of the world where you can witness this phenomenon. Life has a natural rhythm to it, and we are no stranger to the natural flow of its many running waters. Here's the fun part, once we look around and witness the never ending circles that surround us, we can either choose to go with the flow and work with this amazing energy, or fight it and run aimlessly like you're on a hamster wheel.

How about this? Instead of picturing the cycles of life like a giant circle, I'd love for you to imagine a vortex, not unlike a tornado. Even though experiences in life do come "full circle" they never come back to the same beginning. You start from birth and your experiences all come back around but when they do you have learned SO MUCH during that time. So instead of ending a phase and starting all over, you start a new ring, phase or circle, knowing a little more than you did before; making your energy a little bit higher in the vortex.

How can we work with the natural cycles to helps us grow spiritually, emotionally, physically?

The Moon

For the ladies reading this, did you know that our monthly cycles also used to be called our "moon times"? Usually women "flowed" together and that time coordinated with either the new moon or the full moon. If you actually check out a lunar calendar you might be surprised to find that this holds true for you today. Even if you have whacky cycles... there might be some consistency with the moon phases. If this isn't the case, there's nothing weird about you or anything, it's just an interesting thing to take note of.

As you know, the moon has cycles just as we do. We go from new moon (waxing) to crescent, to full (waning) and back again. Does this effect us? Absolutely. My mother worked in a nursing home and told me that she always knew it was a full moon when the residents started acting a little funky. She never quite got into any details about it but I can only imagine what she must have meant! I'm sure you've heard stories about how the energy of the moon affects people. As you probably know the word "luna" is the latin term for "moon". How about the word lunatic? Luna-tic. Apparently whoever developed the word also witnessed some craziness in people around the time of the full moon. We also mustn't leave out the moon lovin' werewolves too, can't forget those!

Seriously though, the ocean's tide is created by the pull of the moon. If our bodies are made up of a large percentage of water then it's pretty likely that bright white thing up in the sky must have an effect on us as well.

Many moons ago (ha!), people have relied on the phases of the moon to help them get through life by means of: farming during the harvest moon, planting during the phases leading up to the full moon, taking care of their animals, choosing when to have babies and most every other part of life one can imagine!

Certain holidays and celebrations from just about every religion are based around the moon phases as well. There is a ton of folklore out there that exists ranging from common sense and interesting such as seeing a ring around the moon at night to foretell troubled energy or weather coming—to hopeful acts like seeing the new moon over your right shoulder will grant your deepest wish. Then there's the downright silly superstitions like cutting your hair during the waning moon will promote baldness, so never cut your hair after the full moon... or something. That kind of thing makes me really wonder how people come up with this stuff!

"Working with the Moon Phases"

If you try to Google this subject you will come across a TON of different ways to work with the moon phases. Since this entire book has been written based on things that I've experimented and experienced then that's all I'm going to include.

*It's up to research if you find any of these subjects interesting... because we all love homework right?

Maybe I sound as nutty as the old superstitions but I'm not the only one who believes in using the phases of the moon to create change! Sometimes I just get so caught up with the kids, house, clients, that I forget what an extremely powerful tool the energy of the moon is. That is until I look up in the sky on a star filled summer night while I'm selling cd's and t-shirts at one of my husbands outdoor music concerts and there she is, that beautiful white goddess up there beckoning me to talk to her and let her help me with whatever issues I have going on at the time.

Funny though, because whenever I look up at the full moon I can ALWAYS see a man's face. Maybe it's my part of the hemisphere that makes this so easy to see? Maybe it's the universe simply showing me the duality in everything... there's that word again. Balance! Yay!

New Moon

I feel like the new moon is the most under rated of the moon phases. It just sits up there in the sky all dark-like and no one seems to notice its presence. Animals don't howl at it, it doesn't light the way for sailors or invoke sultry love song lyrics. It seems to go relatively unnoticed by most of us. Until now. :)

When the new moon takes its turn in the night sky, we can see it as a time of reflection and of manifestation. It's a time to look at the dark side of yourself, your fears, your worries, and/or whatever other feeling that you hold deep inside of yourself and change them into something that is positive, uplifting and rewarding.

When you think of your "dark side" I'm sure what comes to mind is a bad decision you made, past mistakes, Luke Skywalker, certain view points or outlooks you have that may seem unfavorable to some, or something else inherently "negative". Really though, our dark sides don't have to illicit bad feelings. Perhaps all of that dark stuff is just like a special type of armor that protects the very core of our beings, our spirit.

Hidden within every single one us is a little flame that represents our very nature, our life's purpose, our reason to be here, our personal drive. It is way deep in there just waiting to be attended to. The flame could be your life's calling that you may have been ignoring or don't know how to get to, it could be an inert passion for something that you don't want to/are too afraid explore. The darkness that surrounds it is made out of fear, severe lack of self confidence, constant judging of other people and comparing them to yourself or some other obstacle that keeps you from reaching that little light inside. When we are too afraid to look inside of ourselves and acknowledge the dark side then we miss out on the opportunity to uncover obstacles that get in the way of us reaching our truest potentials.Therefore, if we won't reach deep enough and acknowledge our faults and partner our spiritual selves with that which is so mundanely human, then there's no way to break through that wall, that armor, that protects the light of our lives.

By not recognizing your WHOLE being— good and bad, dark and light, surface only, then you may be finding yourself wishing for specific material things or changes and becoming depressed because they never happen. You then find yourself stuck in a vicious circle that repeats itself continuously as opposed to that vortex I mentioned before that slowly brings your cycles higher and higher and higher towards happiness and fulfillment.

The new moon is a time to stop wishing for change and to physically, mentally, and emotionally do something about it. In the words of my wonderful and funny father, "Wish in one hand and sh-t in the other, and see which one you get first." A little grodie, yes, but painfully true. We can wish, wish, wish until all the stars fall out of the sky but sometimes that energy just isn't enough to get what you truly want. It's by taking another baby step and trying to take action that creates the momentum to propel you forward.

Remember that in the beginning it's always dark, so you have to decide which you want to be, the raging fire or the eternal flame.

Steps for Change

Write, Rite, Right

A rite is a ritual. Lemme guess…when you think of rituals you probably imagine lighting colored candles, chanting, and dancing to ethereal sounding music in the nude. Or maybe that's just what I think? In any event, while that kind of ritual can be entertaining, that's not quite the type of ritual that I'm addressing here. Performing a ritual can be empowering, motivational, and moving. It centers your being and prepares you mentally, physically, and energetically for accomplishing whatever outcome you are working towards. The type of ritual for harnessing the moon energy I'm referring to here is writing. Yes, writing can be grounding, centering, calming, and just as spiritually uplifting as dancing naked under the full moon. Joy!

A few key things you can do to heighten your ritualistic writing experience:

1. Write when it is QUIET. If that's possible. After the babies are in bed is a good time. Unless, you're like me and need that time to get other things done or just stare into space to reboot after a long day. Nap time is also good. Before anyone gets up in the morning, or during long late night feeding sessions.
2. Candles. Not necessary honestly, but they certainly create a sacred type of atmosphere. They can be a specific color to reflect the mood of what you are writing about, or to represent the goal to which you want to manifest. (ex. I want to bring more positive energy to our lives so I will light a bright sunny orange candle. I'm trying to find an affordable sitter so I will light a green candle, etc.)
3. Incense. Again not necessary but another one of those sacred space mood enhancers. The smoke does have a clearing affect and diverse scents do create different moods and energies. You can experiment with these or leave them out. Especially if you're allergic or have a little one in the room with you. Or a curious cat. Yeah, definitely keep incense and candles away from cats. I had a cat once who jumped on my kitchen table and stood right over, like belly almost touching, a candle flame. She was totally oblivious, and I almost had a heart attack thinking she must have badly burned herself. After I grabbed her and wafted away the singed cat hair smell, she turned out to be just fine!

4. Turn off the phone, computer, television, and any outside stimulation so you can focus your attention and not be buzzed by all the electric energy around you.
5. Music is your friend. I LOVE creating ambiance with music. Use it happily if you are a fan. If not, keep it off. No biggie.
6. Don't forget to relax, breathe, and enjoy this moment of you time!

Old Fashion Pen and Paper

Really... who uses these ancient tools anymore? I use my smartphone to take notes, write grocery lists and fly the kids to school. For this exercise, I'm asking you to raid the bottom of your junk drawers (or take out the notebook you've been working with) get a pen, a piece of paper, your dreams, and be ready to write!

Start by making a list of all the things that you want to bring into your life. This can be done during any moon phase of course, but it can be particularly effective during the new moon. No list is too big, too silly or too needy. Just write, write, write until you get that little bump on your middle finger from too much pen to skin friction.

When you're done, take your list and prioritize. What do you need most in your life right now? Notice I said need. What do you NEED to help you right now. Take those things and circle them.

Next, underline the things that you want right now. To give you an idea of what I mean, a need is something that you really can't live without. OMG I NEED a haircut! Oh man I really need to pay this bill! My car is about to fall apart, I need a new one! You get the idea.

A WANT is something you want. Duh, Jen. Okay, a want is something that isn't a necessity but has the potential to make you happy. I really want a manicure because my nails look like crap and it would make me feel better. I want to buy my kids an ipod because they keep stealing my phone. I want to send my kids to camp because they're driving me crazy over summer vacation (just kidding). How about: I want to find a way to go camping with the kids over summer vacation because they'd love it. There, that's way better. :) Now take the three most important things from both lists and write them out on another piece of paper.

Done! Almost.

You can do a number of things with your list:
1. You can read them out loud once a day until the full moon, where you'll give up your list for another one about "letting go."
2. Take that piece of paper, find a fire proof container, campfire, or something that will not burn your house down or cause you personal harm and then burn the list. The act of burning intentions goes way

back to like, well way before one of the Jonas Brother's got his own reality TV shows. ;) The idea is that your intention goes up in the burning smoke to be sent to god or the divine. But also so you don't dwell on these things. It's kind of like an egg timer that you can set and forget. This act can be a powerful form of manifestation. It allows you to confront what you really need, bring in some fun wants, and send them out to the universe and AWAY from your control. In essence, it keeps you from worrying about things.

3. Bury the list. Let the earth soak in your intentions and turn that piece of paper into mulch. A win, win.

4. Put it somewhere in your house where you'll be reminded. Tape it to your bathroom mirror, onto the bag of cat or dog food, your coffee maker, or where ever you are sure to see it. This is to remind yourself that thoughts are things and if you put the thought out there it will come back to you in physical form.

5. Meditate. You might have to make a shorter list for this though so you don't forget what you wrote. If you do happen to forget what you wrote, maybe it's a sign you don't really need that thing anyway, right? Cheers!

Meditation

Meditation is my go to for just about everything, as you know, and manifesting with the new moon via meditation is no exception. It just feels like whether you are writing things down or meditating to bring change that you are DOING something about your issues instead of wishing them away. Do you know what I mean? Sometimes when you feel like you can't do anything about your problems you get stuck, feel sad, and well…downright hopeless. At least in this way, you are contributing to change instead of waiting for change to happen. On that note, here's a meditation for you to try.

Again, it might help to record yourself saying this meditation and playing it back. Alternately, you can familiarize yourself with the meditation and do it on your own with soft music playing, or be lulled by the middle of the night sounds the sound of your babies' deep breathing.

New Moon Meditation

1. Have up to three items from your list in mind. You can do more or less depending on your necessities and how much you can handle remembering.
2. Get in your comfy spot where you won't be bothered for a few minutes.
3. Close your eyes.
4. Take a few deep breaths in through your nose and out through your mouth.
5. Relax!
6. Imagine you are on a beach and it is dark out. It is the new moon so only the stars act as lights for you.
7. You know in your mind that you are completely safe and comfortable here.
8. Slowly scan your surroundings and make a mental note of what you see here.
9. Right along the shoreline you notice a set of stairs that extends way high into the night sky.
10. The stairs are there for a purpose, to help you reach the new moon, and give your intentions directly to the source.
11. As you approach this staircase, you notice that just at the bottom there is a small box. You look at the details of the box, the size, shape, and color. You are amazed at how light weight it is as well.
12. Instinctively, you know that this box has a special purpose. It is there to help you carry your intentions to the new moon.
13. With intentions in mind you open the empty box and either whisper them into your box or place your list inside of it.
14. When you are done, close your box and tuck it away under your arm.
15. Now take the first step up the stairs.
16. You slowly ascend the stairs knowing the walk up to the moon will be effortless to that point that you aren't really walking so much as gliding higher and higher.
17. You are not afraid, you know you are completely safe and almost feel giddy as you ascend feeling a slight breeze on your face.
18. You notice shapes in the clouds as you go past them. What are the shapes? Can you see anything below you? Be aware of your surroundings as you climb.
19. You see that you are nearing the top and you slow your climb now until you reach the last step.

20. You've made it. In front of you now is a platform that you are safe to walk on and very close ahead is the new moon itself! Don't be alarmed if it doesn't appear as a moon, it could be anything at all. It could be a person, an animal, a plant, or some other random object. Just know that it is there for you to help manifest your intentions!

21. Walk over now to the moon and lay your box down in front of it. You may wish to recite your intentions again or even talk to it for a little while. You never know, she/he/it may just have something nice to say to you!

22. After you feel you've spent enough time, express your gratitude for having been heard.

23. It's time to walk back to your staircase and descend slowly down until you reach your beautiful beach.

24. Touch the sand with both hands and feel its grittiness between your fingers. Take a deep breath and fill your heart with joy knowing you are going to manifest your dreams!

25. Take another deep breath and open your eyes.

26. Write everything in your journal or talk it out on your smart phone's recorder.

***

So... what did you think? I bet that experience was chalk full of symbolism, huh? The first time I tried this meditation for myself, the moon did not appear to me as a moon. It was a lady wearing a long black dress with matching veil that covered her flowing black hair. She didn't say anything just presented me with a warm smile...it was pretty neat. That's why I said to not be surprised if there is no moon there at all, the energy you are creating will manifest itself in a way that is right and meaningful (or super bizarre) to you.

I also wanted to add that, if you want, there is a variation of this meditation. I didn't include it in the above steps because I figured there is enough info in there to boggle your mind. If you work with this for a little while and decide you want to add more then go ahead and try this step:

24 1/2. After you arrive back on the sandy beach at the bottom of the staircase, you are pleasantly surprised to find the very same box you gave to the moon! Open it now, and see what was put inside for you. It is a unique and special message, just for you! Express your gratitude in any way that you see fit. Reach down and touch the sand beneath you with both hands and feel its grittiness between your fingers. Take a deep breath and fill your heart with joy knowing you are going to manifest your dreams!

This meditation can be used any time you want. You can even substitute the moon for something else if you desire. Maybe you want to meet your spirit guide. You can go in with the intention that your spirit guide is at the top of the stairs, waiting to chat with you. Your totem animal could be up there, the answer to a burning question could be up there as well. USE your imagination and TRUST your intuition. Of course, do not forget to write it down, you may be amazed with the answers you receive or the feelings that you express at the time, when reading back through at a later date.

I'm a huge advocate for lists/writing things down and meditation so those are my top two for working with the new moon energy. I hope you find that one of the above exercises makes a difference for you!

Full Moon

As we know, the full moon takes all of the night time press. Everyone has heard songs, stories, or has a tale of their own to tell about it. What makes it so special on a spiritual level? This phase creates enormous energy geared towards letting things go. Ever watch that show *Hoarders*? Now those people could use a gigantic helping of full moon energy.

Often times we hang on to things that no longer serve our purpose and this makes us feel stuck, sad, lonely, confused, or other ranges of emotions that we can't seem to put our fingers on. We just know that we feel completely off or out of balance. If you are human then chances are you carry around some sort of emotional baggage that weighs you down in some way. Or not. Honestly every person is so entirely different and unique. Some handle different emotional environments and life transitions with ease, while it feels as though those same types of situations take control of others.

Whichever way you go, I'll bet there is something in your life that you need to let go of. It could be a relationship that you've been stuck in and can't get yourself out of, a fear that is keeping you from doing what you really want (like you don't believe in yourself enough for insert absurd reason here) having trouble accepting your present situation, and so on.

There is a saying I've often heard in my life. "Let Be and Let God." Too often we have issues with control. We want everything the way we want them and wont accept that there are other plans for us. Well doesn't THAT get shot to hades when we have kids?

The full moon energy helps us to bring the control back into our lives by giving us permission to let go of that which no longer serves our purposes or holds our best interests at heart. It is also a time to energize our bodies and our minds! At the new moon we set intentions to better ourselves. The full moon is a time to let go of that which is holding us back and set those intentions into action! Or just to allow a really awesome energy cleanse of our whole beings: mind, body, and spirit.

The Mighty Pen

You can work with the full moon pretty much the same way that you can the new moon, using the same types of writing exercises I had mentioned. With the full moon, however, you have to search your heart and figure out what it is in your life that you <u>need to let go of.</u>

The difference between these suggestions and that of the new moon is that with the new moon you want to manifest so you want to see those papers with your intentions and hang on to them. If not physically, then with your heart or your imagination. You want to give your intentions enough energy to appear here for you in the physical world.

On the full moon, you are letting go. That means I don't want to see you hanging on to those pieces of paper. I want to see you safely burn the paper, bury it in the earth, have the kids make shreds of confetti out of it or whatever other creative way you can think to release the energy contained on the paper. Just do it big! The bigger the better—as long as it is safe and you don't hurt anyone or yourself in the process. And, of course, have fun with it. Remember the movie, *Monsters Inc.* when they discovered that laughter creates way more energy then tears? I think they were on to something there!

Always try and enjoy what you are doing!

Moon Flower Meditation

Okay I'll admit it, this meditation has a girly title but that doesn't mean you fellas out there can't work with it. Like it or not, you guys have female energy in there too! It's all about balance, right?

I wrote a variation of this meditation while preparing to teach a Reiki level one class to help raise the energy vibration of my students and they had such amazing experiences with it, I thought it'd be a fine idea to tweak it to fit our purposes here. My goal with this meditation is to raise your energy, make you feel energized, feel your inner light, and empower you to complete your goals and know in your heart you have the power to live your dreams. It's not as far fetched as it sounds!

Moon Flower Meditation

1. Take a couple of deep breaths, in through your nose and out through your mouth.
2. Imagine that you are the bud of a beautiful white moon flower at early dusk. You are not yet open, not yet able to see.
3. You feel deeply that you are apart of something but you don't exactly know what it is.
4. You feel your roots snuggling deeply with the earth's soil.
5. You feel the energy around you and smell the evening air full of fresh cut grass, sweet flowers, and outdoor grills burning out after dinner.
6. You are content in this blind yet fascinating place.
7. You notice that the world around you appears to be getting darker. There is a slight chill in the air, and a silence from human noises as they close their doors and windows.
8. All that surrounds your auditory senses now is the gentle hum of crickets, the chirp of toads searching for their mates, the rustle of wind as it caresses darkened leaves, and all of the other natural sounds that come out at night.
9. You feel and sense a cool white glow as the moon rises high in the sky. It is her light that touches the outer part of your body, trying to penetrate to the core of your being.
10. As the beam of moonlight becomes stronger, it begins to touch your soul, igniting a dormant spark inside of you.
11. Feel your entire being, your mind, body, and spirit, fill completely with love and white light of the moon.
12. You are enamored and empowered by this light which has suddenly entered your dark and content existence.

13. As if a child discovering magic for the first time, your heart fills with so much curiosity and joy that you allow it to burst open exposing your true and inner beauty!
14. You are now a white moon flower, open, alive, and viewing your world with brand new senses that didn't exist until now. You look around and see you are not alone, after all. You see that you have a place among family, friends, acquaintances, and strangers— other flowers that stand together connected by roots and stems, leaves, and branches, all apart of the same bushes, yet shining in the beauty of individuality.
15. You are proud of your individual beauty and strength, basking in the cool glow that only the full moon can give you. You are a new flower, vibrant, alive, and deeply connected to those around you, and to mother earth herself.
16. Bask in the knowledge now, that there is a beautiful being inside of you that is empowering and can be self-empowered to do as you dream. Know that when your petals opened, you lost all that no longer serves your purpose. Dare now to reel in the new energy and to live with the knowledge that all that seemed impossible before is possible now.
17. When you are ready, take a couple of deep breaths and come back into the room.

***

What did you think of that one? I hope you had an incredible eye opening experience! If not, that's okay. Try again or let it be. That's part of the beauty of *Finding Your Spirit*. You find YOUR spirit, not mine. I hope you wrote or recorded your experiences to delve into at a later time. Always remember that sometimes we feel like the bud and other times we feel like the flower as our energy waxes and wanes from hour to hour, day to day.

Don't fight how you feel, just roll with it kicking it up a notch anytime you see fit.

LIVING WITHIN THE SEASONS

I swear Stephanie Mayer should have written the *Twilight* books based on my hometown. Those vampires would never sparkle here, that's for darn sure. There is a pretty solid six month period during the fall-winter-spring combo where we rarely ever see the sun and the sky opens up to dump buckets of snow on us. You'd think that would make for reasonably good snowboarding or skiing, right? Well, it doesn't. The hills are usually half iced over and packed through, making your ass landings particularly painful. Oh the joy of living near the Great Lakes!

Our weather seems to coincide with the old saying, "Sh#t or get off the pot." To sum it up, we live with it or move down south. I'm sure every region has their woes though and we all deal with them one way or the other. We can learn a lot from the different seasons if we open ourselves up to the possibilities they can bring. It's not just about amazing or crappy weather. It's about witnessing life cycles, embracing change, and even feeling the energy of the earth.

In the following pages I've broken down the seasons and emphasized the importance of living in the present moment as a means to stay spiritually grounded, balance, and connected.

** In Fall of 2013, I challenged myself to "Live Within The Seasons" by trying to do something fall related EVERY day through the the months of September, October, November, part of December and blogged about it. Sometimes the experiences were funny, other times they were more reflective. I even tried my hand at being crafty which is quite a feat for me. I'm not anti crafty... I am uncrafty, but it was fun just the same. The results of my seasonal experiment changed my perspective on a lot of things. I learned that you don't have to try so hard to live in the moment, you just have to stop what you are doing, pick your head up, and view the world with all of your senses. I encourage anyone willing to try the challenge to go ahead and do it. I'd love to hear your results!

Now… let's see what embracing the seasons and living in the present moment can do for our wellbeing!

Fall

I've said it before, but if you are lucky enough to live in a part of the country where the seasons actually change then embrace the beauty of each season when you can. Even the long cold winters have their own special magic, if you change the way you think about them. If you don't, still get out and really observe what each season has to offer. Here in the Northeast, our fall is magical! The air becomes crisp, the leaves change, there are apples to pick, pumpkin patches, soup, chili, dark beer....

We can use the seasons like a wheel to help us grow holistically where each season represents one giant turn until we come right back to the beginning, starting with Autumn which represents "harvest".

Traditionally during this time of year, families would can, store, and prepare their food supplies for the long winters. Animals and people readied themselves for the cold road ahead and hunkered down to prepare for what came next. Whether for hibernation or the extensive nap the earth takes each year, the energy is at its peak during this time and slowly starts to wane and freeze over. Okay sometimes not so slowly... once in awhile we get those, "Hey look the leaves are starting to change color but it's still warm—holy crap it's a blizzard" type of years but you know, we work with what we have.

This time of year is PERFECT for cleaning house. *Eat your heart out spring cleaning, fall is way better for this!* Of course you can do it again in the spring to let the new air in but fall really is the best for this.

Seriously, why wait? If you're going to be stuck inside all winter why not be stuck somewhere that is comfortable? I'm not just talking physically either. The fall is a time to harvest your inner stuff, to take note of what is going on in your life, and to acknowledge and clean your spiritual house, too. You can use a lot of the same steps as I mentioned in the section on working with the moon phases to do this.

Here are some other suggestions to take advantage of this peaking seasonal energy:

1. On the first day of fall or just whenever during the fall months, make that priority list, release the emotions, relationships, whatevers, that no longer serve your purpose.
2. Manifest your desires. Make a list of everything positive you want to bring into your life.
3. Make a happy list. Think of all the things that make you happiest and write them down.
4. Get a calendar and start planning things that you have been putting off like playdates, little trips to see friends, family, or just an adventure with the kids.
5. Make a sad list. Write down everything that is bumming you out, then burn it! (in a safe place, of course)
6. Organize everything! Clean the house, get a mani and pedi if you can, create a sacred space or corner in your house for meditation. (Closets work too!)
7. Most importantly, stop putting things off. Make that trip to the doctors office or dentist that you should've gone to six months ago. Allow anything that has been weighing heavily on your shoulders to be acknowledged and do something about it.
8. Live completely in the moment, take a ride out in nature and see the transformation that is taking place.
9. Craft with the kids. Autumn is a wonderful thing for your creativity. With all the changes taking place—the colors, and cooler air, you really are left open to create something amazing with a seasonal theme. Collect leaves, little pumpkins, rocks and sticks. Paint them, glue them, let your creativity loose!
10. Food, food, and more food. It's harvest season after all and now is a good time to buy up that winter squash and prepare meals that warm your body and satisfy the belly!

***

Those are a few of the things that you can do to clean all of your houses during the fall season—to harvest the good and abundant energy and clear away the yuck. When it's all said and done you will be way prepared for the winter and hopefully will feel soooooo much better!

Winter

My own personal feelings about winter goes like this: Let it snow until New Years and then bring on the sunshine! But that doesn't happen here. Oh no... I'm a May baby and there have been many occasions where I got snow as a birthday present. Yeah, the snow thing loses its magic pretty quickly so what can you do to keep your cool (hardy, har) and maintain balance during the long dark winter?

Of course vacation comes to mind. If you can't afford a vacation then I would even like to say go out and make the most of it, but I would be kidding myself if I said that. Just because it's cold and dark doesn't always mean there is snow. It could mean that there is freezing rain, plain rain, or nothing but cold and darkness. Well now that I've written the two most depressing paragraphs in history, let's really figure out how to make the most of winter!

1. Start by observing what happens to the earth during this time. Next, observe what is going on with your body. Take note of how you feel. Finally, compare your findings between what is going on in nature to what is happening to your own body. It's neat to see that there are similarities between the two. If you become depressed during the winter, this experiment may help you to understand that this is the natural rhythm of life. You'll find (if you haven't noticed already) that your mood will pass just as the weather does and will brighten again when the sun comes back. If you do this once a week or make a regular routine of it, you'll probably be able to catch the very first sprouts of spring that you might have missed without presently observing. Seeing new life in any form is usually the best pick me up, ever! Do this with your kids too. They always think I'm nuts when I squeeeee! over a new flower popping out of the snow. It brings me great joy to keep them guessing when Mommy's going to lose it once and for all. :)
2. Treat the whole winter season just as you would the new moon and use it to manifest, manifest, manifest. Go back to all of the tools I listed for working with the new moon and try them out during the winter as well. I definitely see new moon time to be bff's with the winter for obvious reasons. The winter is dark and cold and well...

wintry, the new moon is dark and uhh...dark! It's a wonderful time to build that manifesting moment for a big release in spring time.

3. Try and create a vision board of all the things you want to bring into your life, places you want to go, things that keep you happiest and put it somewhere you can see it every day. It's a great project for the kids, too!

4. Use this time as an excuse to have more playdates, host company, and be with family beyond the whole holiday thing. We naturally want to stay indoors during this time and why go at it alone? Unless you can't stand your family and can only really tolerate them during the holidays. This is a time to stop making excuses and start making plans for visits with friends that you haven't spoken to in awhile. It's a time to surround yourself with people that lift your spirits.

5. Just as in the new moon, this is a fabulous time to do some soul searching and embrace your dark side. Again, with the dark side, I don't mean bad stuff...like if your dark side consists of hurtful thoughts about yourself or others then please go get help. This "dark" side is more about not liking certain things about yourself such as bad habits, or anything that doesn't contribute to your overall happiness.

6. You can also check off the days until spring on your calendar (assuming you still use the ol' pocketbook or wall variety). Make a colorful paper chain and do the same, like those ones we had to make in preschool to countdown Christmas vacation, only prettier. I won't tell anyone that a grown up made them!

Winter is dark and kind of depressing, yes. Some people thrive in the winter though and that's great!! Whether you like it or hate it, we have no control over the seasons, so finding ways to exist within its boundaries, being PROACTIVE about your situation is a wonderful way to keep your spirit soaring.

Spring

Spring, glorious spring. I always feel like doing cartwheels when I see the first purple crocus's pop up from under the snow. Then I feel bad for the little buggers thinking they must be freezing and I get sad knowing they must realize that they probably made a grave mistake by blooming so early and want to shrink back down into their warm homes but can't... and you must think I've gone absolutely apey! Or ducky? All I can picture is myself wandering in circles jumping up and down like Daffy Duck, "Whoo! Whoo! Whoohooo! Whoohoo!"

That's what spring does to me though! It's almost like I can feel myself waking up along with the rest of the earth. The world smells different (like mud and sweet hyacinths) the sun is a little warmer, and people decide to go out in shorts, t-shirts, and sandals on the first 50 degree day. Yes, I'm serious. This group does not include myself, I assure you.

The word "spring" is chock full of its own spiritual symbolism, isn't it? You think of sprouts "springing" open. You feel your energy "springing" open. More doors "spring" open as people start to shuffle outside and walk around to enjoy the fresh warm air and windows "spring" open to allow all the new energy into their homes and offices. Baby birds "spring" from their eggs. Animals "spring" awake from hibernation. You get the picture, spring equals new life, new growth, and new opportunities!

This is a particularly good time to do a serious spring cleaning. I know we already talked about the great fall house cleanse to prepare for the coming winter and now would be the time to get rid of the stagnant energy and whatever funky smells made residence throughout the long months. If you don't have a winter, it's a good time to clean anyway. Why not, right?

While you are cleansing your house, it couldn't hurt to do a body cleanse as well. While showers and baths are good and hopefully you take them on a regular basis, that's not what I'm talking about here. Take stock of your fridge and kitchen items. It's probably overflowing with fresh fruits and vegetables, right? Ok, ok, ok, maybe your "fresh foods" entails a single brown banana sitting on the kitchen counter. You can sort of include that in your list... freeze that banana and blend it later to make dairy free ice cream! (Peel it first though, I learned the hard way that you need to do that before you freeze it. Doh!)

This time of year is when you see the freshest locally grown fruits and vegetables appearing on the shelves and outdoor markets. Do yourself a favor and hit up these places to restock and refresh your body. It's usually way less expensive than what some of the major grocery stores offer and a lot safer too, as in most local farmers refrain from using scary chemicals that do not wash off. Plus it's awesome for the local economy to support businesses that thrive in your own backyard.

Here are some other things you can do to take advantage of springtime energy:

1. Plant a garden in your yard. If you don't have a yard, get a big flower pot and grow some veggies in there. Create an herb garden. Have the kids help, they love to see the new sprouts grow and might even be inclined to eat the vegetables that they actually grew themselves.
2. Go for nature walks alone or with your critters. Really breathe deeply and take in all of what spring has to offer through all of your senses. It is very grounding and energizing at the same time.
3. Start something new, like a hobby.
4. This is another good time to release unwanted energies, old habits, whatever no longer serves your purpose.
5. Eat fresh, locally grown food.
6. Holidays are not the only times to give back, donate, or help the less fortunate. Use the springtime energy of abundance to help those in need. Make it a ritual to volunteer on the first day of spring. Bring a basket of flowers to a neighbor or some other random act of kindness.
7. Go to a local farm or zoo with the kids and show them all the baby animals, explain how spring represents new life and growth.
8. Go crazy with paint using spring colors!
9. Meditate. A simple and effective meditation would be to sit outside (if you can) and breath deeply the smells of the earth, feeling the warm sun on your face. Thank the universe/god/etc. for the new life that you are witnessing and for your blessings. Feel your energy rise and expand. Bask in the clean energy and close your meditation feeling refreshed and full of love/gratitude.
10. Look in the mirror and pick two things that you love about yourself. Say them out loud, every day. Pick two things about your significant other that you love and tell them. Do this for your kids as well.
11. Take full advantage of the love energy that is spring!

What other ways can you think of to take advantage of the spring energy?

Summer

I have so many amazing memories of summer as a kid; picnics on the Fourth of July with my family, fireworks, swimming pools, camping, no school. Truth be told one of my favorite smells is fresh black tar settling after a new driveway or parking lot has been put in. Sometimes you can catch the smell when driving by a construction site on the road. I don't exactly remember where I was or why I got to do this but I can recall sitting on the side of a driveway (Maybe it was my own? Who knows) and poking the tar bubbles that kept popping up from the heat—like a black, gooey, noiseless version of bubble wrap. Hours of entertainment!

Now being all grown up and stuff summer has a totally different feeling, as you know. I can definitely relive some of those memories through my kids when they go out hunting for toads, watching them swim (the kids, not the toads), run through sprinklers, and get soooooooo excited when they hear the bell of the ice cream truck. My youngest totally fell over in the front yard this summer because he got all worked up that he was going to miss the ice cream man. I think he definitely takes after my lack of coordination. Poor kid.

Young or old summer has a way of sneaking its nostalgia into your pores. Let's take a look at how we can take advantage of the energy and bring the spirit back into the season.

Spiritual Summer

1. Walk barefoot in the grass or the beach. It feels sooo good to kick off your shoes and run around in the grass or squish sand between your toes. Just steer clear of clover. I recently stepped on a bee because I figured I would be safe since it just rained. Needless to say in the battle between Mom vs Bee... bee won. Well the stinger won. The poor bee, not so much.
2. Just as in the spring, enjoy locally grown food as often as possible.
3. Herb gardens can be planted now, too. Put them in a pot that allows you to bring them in and out of the house so you can keep them in the winter.
4. Make sun tea. Drop a few teabags in a pitcher, cover, and leave in the sun for a few hours to brew.
5. Home made popsicles with fresh fruit for the kids. Make grown up versions with vodka or rum when you've had a particularly rough day. ;)
6. If you have the means to get out for a family trip to a park, camping, or whatever, do it! Sometimes all you need to break up energy is a change of scenery.
7. If you have a yard, get a chiminea or a fire pit. Fire is super mesmerizing and meditative. It warms your family and forces everyone to sit around and talk to each other. Unless you are like me — I cannot sit around the fire. I hover because the smoke follows me no matter where I go. It's a joke in my house that no one wants to sit next to me because they'll get smoked out, too!
8. Zen your way to the beach. Lay in the sand, listen to the waves, and allow your spirit to soar, let the sun "burn" off negativity or blocks in your energy. Also, build labyrinths or castles in the sand. (Remember to protect your skin with sunblock!)
9. Road trips to the country.
10. Hike in the woods.

Need I continue? The best thing about summer is that it is so easy to get out there and enjoy nature in every way possible. Summer time is about togetherness, exploration, discovery, and gratitude, so take full advantage of what lies right in front of you during this season. Live in the moment, in the present during this time (and as often as you can). Summer reminds us that life is being lived and enjoyed all around us. We can either join the party or not. I choose to be a joiner. How about you?

After contemplating an entire turn of the seasonal wheel, can you see now that that we never finish at the same point we started? Life exists in a series of circles that spin like a vortex, coming back around and allowing you to move to a higher plane or place in life.

Try some of the exercises in this chapter by working with the moon or living within the seasons and see how they resonate with you. Try to manifest a dream or two, let go of unwanted energies in your life, feel your heart open up, live within your individual cycles. Remember that there is only one of you. There is no one else like you on this planet. Even if you are a twin! You deserve to let that uniqueness shine in every way possible.

Celebrate each circle of your life's vortex!

HOLISTICALLY SPEAKING

Throughout this book I give lots of exercises to help you take care of the spiritual aspect of your being. We delve into meditation, symbolism, intuition, tools, chakras, lions and tigers and bears (oh my!). That last bit was supposed to be a joke but now that I think about it, I do discuss totem animals in here— spirit does have a sense of humor!

I also challenge your mind by encouraging you to think outside of the box and explore your creativity. I suggest that you feed your hungry brain by researching the subjects that strike your fancy and offer mental respites through relaxation and meditation exercises—because brains get tired, too.

In order to complete the holistic circle here, I wanted to dive into something that has probably been completely forgotten about since you brought home your pink or blue bundles of joy.

Your body!

Does thinking about the word "body" make you say, "Ugh. Don't even get me started?"

It certainly did for me after I had the boys. When I was pregnant, I couldn't believe how every part and I mean EVERY part of my body could stretch past maximum capacity. Especially towards my due date, I thought if my stomach was going to get any larger then the baby was just going to pop through my belly button. Post pregnancy I had some fantastical notion that my balloon belly would automatically deflate back down to pre pregnant position. Yeah…no. That didn't happen—and the boobs…forget it. Let's just say they're not as perky as they used to be.

You know what, though? I'm proud of my post pregnancy body and you should be too! I won't go into the debatable mess about societal expectations of body image right now but know that your body is beautiful no matter what. The stretch marks, belly hang, droopy boobs, cellulite and varicose veins all mean that you took care of yourself to make sure that you would give birth to the healthiest baby possible. Good job, gorgeous Mama!

On the flip side, if you never were pregnant because you adopted or are a daddy, then your body most likely is still the same but I bet you don't have time to take care of or even think about it the way you did before you became a parent. Am I right?

In whatever parental category you fall into please know that taking care of your body needs to be put back onto your priority list. You simply can't maintain a spiritually balanced lifestyle without respecting that gorgeous human shell of yours! Not to mention, you need to maintain your energy and strength when catering to the many demands of wee ones and ya can't do that unless your body is healthy!

Your body is the incredible home to your mind and spirit. Without your body, you would just be a spirit. Without the mind your body wouldn't thrive. Without the spirit you would just… exist. That's why we call it the "mind-body-spirit" connection. You need to keep all three of those things in check to maintain your balance as an individual, caregiver and spiritual person.

Pac-Man: Feed The Belly

I'm not a doctor or nutritionist—just a lady who's been around this holistic thing for awhile and has learned a thing or two to share. I can't tell you the best foods for postpartum recovery or what to consume that will increase your breast milk. I can only remind you of something simple that you learned a very long time ago.

YOU. NEED. TO. EAT.

That sounds so mundane and obvious doesn't it? Well, in the very early days of parenthood eating is something I would forget quite often. It usually wasn't until I found myself dumping banana baby puffs straight into my mouth from the plastic can that I realized how hungry I was and let me tell you those things are not very filling! I wish I would have known what it was like to have a newborn before I had one. Lucky for you that my mistakes are your learning opportunities!

Here are a couple of thought starters to help make sure you get proper nourishment in the beginning:

Plan Ahead
1. Have the numbers to every food delivery service on the contacts in your phone. In the section where you can add notes, include their healthiest meal options. That way you can just dial and order without having to deal with finding and reading through a menu.
2. Make and freeze meals.
3. Enlist the help of family members and neighbors.

Even if your babies are a little older and you have free reign over the kitchen cupboards then it might do you some good to plan ahead instead of cooking for the kids and scarfing down their leftovers. I've seen some really cool ideas on Pinterest where people make healthy grab and go snacks in plastic containers and leave them in the fridge to just... "grab and go." A little time consuming yes, but not at a bad idea. Actually I think I'm just writing all this so I remember to do it, too. ;)

Also, when planning your grocery list remember that healthy doesn't hurt. I always tell my boys to treat people the way they would want to be treated themselves. I think we can extend that same lesson to what we ingest into our bodies. Treat your body the way you want to be treated. Would you rather be coated in a layer of salty florescent orange… stuff… or be lathered in healing vitamins and minerals? The answer is a no brainer for me— bring on the banana lotion! Okay kidding, slathering myself in bananas would be pretty disgusting but I think you see my point here.

One other suggestion I have is to keep a food diary—another use for that pesky journal I asked you to keep. For three days, try writing down every bite of food that you put in your mouth. Include the type of food and the time you ate it. Even if it's half of a stolen package of Baby Mum Mum's, write it down. At the end of the third day, go back and look at your food diary. Sometimes we just don't realize how little, how much, or what we are eating! Keeping a food diary can really make a difference —it helps you to identify trigger eating, problem areas, and may shed light on where you might need to make a nutritional adjustment.

I know it sounds a little silly to dedicate so many words on remembering to eat but it truly is important to keep you balanced, focused, energized, and healthy!

Let's Get Physical

Some people love it, others hate it. No matter which side of the see saw you sit on, it's undeniable that our bodies were made to be physically fit. These days, however, it's not like we are in the wild foraging for food unless you try shopping at Wegmans the day before a major holiday—so most of us have to work a little harder to stay in shape. Whether it's a gym membership, yoga classes, or Jane Fonda exercises at home, it helps to establish a routine that we can realistically follow.

Exercise came a little easier for me when I lived in Manhattan. I stayed in shape by shlepping my Phil and Ted's three wheeled double stroller to the grocery store, baby classes, and up and down the subway stairs. Rain or shine it was always walk, walk, climb stairs, walk, walk, run for the subway, walk, walk. Unfortunately that isn't so here in Western, NY. Stores are a little too far away for me to consider walking to, but I try to sneak in the physical fitness whenever and however I can.

Sometimes all you can do is little things to keep yourself physically active as not all of us have a gym membership or treadmills in our offices. Every little bit helps, in my opinion, and if even if you can add a few small changes to your routine, you are not only adding obvious physical health benefits but mental and emotional ones as well.

Here are a few suggestions to add more activity to your daily routine:

1. If you see a Doris Day parking spot (closest to the entrance) at your local grocery store, skip it and let the next person who may have trouble walking, needs assistance, or has a bunch of babies in the car, take it. Instead, park further back to give yourself a couple of extra healthy steps to walk and hopefully an easier time getting out of the lot because there's usually more empty spaces in the back.
2. Use the stairs whenever possible. We lived on the 31st floor and I used to try and see how far I could walk, if my husband had the kids and I ran down to do laundry or check the mail. I never made it much past the twelfth floor but dang is stair climbing a good workout!
3. Cleaning. This is a two-fer. Not only do you get a sparkling house, but you can burn those calories at the same time. If *Mrs. Doubtfire* can do it, so can you!
4. Crawl along the floor with the babies. I used to have races with my little crawlies when they were small.

5. Play tag, hide and seek, throw a frisbee around.
6. Go for a bike ride.
7. Walk the kids to school instead of driving them (if you live close enough).
8. Do toe raises while you are washing the dishes.
9. Sit on an exercise ball instead of a chair when working on the computer or watching TV.
10. Watching TV? Get up and do jumping jacks during commercials.

I don't need to tell you the benefits of physical activity, I'm sure you already know. Chances are if you have little ones you are probably getting enough exercise anyway. BUT... just in case, hopefully the short list of suggestions above will help you to start thinking about your own body and what you can do to keep it strong and healthy.

Speaking of healthy, another HUGE deterrent to your health besides a poor diet and no activity is LACK OF SLEEP and let's face it, once we have kids sleep turns into one of those luxuries we used to take for granted. I told you the story about how we actually went and hired a night nurse a couple of times so my husband and I could get a full night of sleep when baby #2 was an infant. If there is a way to share duties or enlist the help of friends once in awhile it's worth it. There's no need to be a superhero, sleep is important! You do most of your healing when you are sleeping. Your batteries recharge and you are better able to handle situations and decision making when you're not sleep deprived.

Of course there's not much you can do on those unexpected nights when the growing pains hit, someone has an accident or a bad dream. If you see a pattern with any of those situations or something else with your kids that can cause a potential lack of sleep for you then I would suggest to acknowledge what is going on and do your best to work with it. You need sleep for your mental, emotional, physical, and spiritual health and your family does too. Do your best to get some rest.

Love Thyself

I know I'm stating the obvious here with this body stuff but I feel like it needed to be said. Often times we are soooooo busy taking care of everyone else that we forget we need to take care of ourselves, too. When you're out shopping for the kids clothes, why not pick up a new skirt, shirt, or pair of socks in your favorite color? Just a little self-help gesture like that can make you feel wonderful! Or am I the only one that benefits from retail therapy?

We also have to remember to appreciate what we have been given. Stand in front of a mirror and pick out one thing that you really love about yourself. Hopefully you have more than one thing, but one will do. Be proud of whatever it is. Your eyes? Your haircolor? Your long legs? Our bodies are super special, important, and the only ones we have.

Do what you can to take care of the whole you. Your mind, spirit, and BODY!

DECRESCENDO
ENERGY MEDICINE: A FLAT ENERGETIC WORLD

I believe it is healthy to be skeptical. Some of us find it easier to dismiss an idea than others but for the most part we don't believe everything we see, read, or are told. Could you imagine what life would be like if we did? We would all be walking around with cootie shots drawn on our hands, fingers constantly crossed, guns loaded with silver bullets on the full moon, our necks adorned with garlic jewelry, while swearing that we would never feed our Mogwais after midnight. Indeed, life would be nothing short of bizarre.

While those examples are definitely on the more extreme side, for some, certain aspects of spirituality can feel just as kooky and would be totally met with the skeptical eye roll, upturned nose, and smoke from the heels as they do the roadrunner cartoon exit as fast as humanly possible.

While I never ran away, I definitely did not believe in a lot of this "woo-woo" stuff until I came face to face with it. Reiki was one of my first experiences into this energetic world which I assumed was flat. I know now that it is round and in constant motion and expands as fast as we can explore it—kind of like the wild west of energy! I believe Reiki works in a similar way to acupuncture and the many other various forms of medicine out there that promotes energy movement and relaxation to stimulate your body's self healing mechanisms. HOW all of these things work still remains an unfortunate mystery and I applaud those scientific explorers that step outside of the box and try to "de-woo woo" this amazing field of medicine.

I explained my introduction to Reiki story in the section of this book about chakras. I can tell you it has been over ten years later and I am still going strong, helping those who ask. It has been a whirlwind for me and has taken me to places I have never thought possible. I've given

Reiki while new life was brought into this world, while lives were at their end, and everything in between. It has been my own personal proof that there is a tangible energetic/spiritual world that exists even though we cannot see it, which is why I felt it was important to share it with you now.

Hopefully by reading and trying some of the exercises within this book, instead of a flat energetic world, you see that it might have some curves, that question marks start to form, and you feel a greater connection to something you can't explain, or maybe you can!

Immersing yourself in spirituality doesn't mean that you have to lose faith in what you already believe in. It doesn't mean that you have to start to believe in something that has always appeared intangible to you. *Finding Your Spirit* is exactly what it sounds like. It's a way to discover what makes YOU tick as an individual. What is that one song that can perk you up no matter how bad you are feeling? What memory can you think of that STILL makes you laugh many years later? What is the one thing that can un-bunch your knickers when you've had a rough day? ALL of those things are unique to only you.

You are matter and you do matter. Remember that!

When you are a parent it becomes really easy to be the soggy Cheerio left in the family bowl. Between work, housekeeping, meal planning, organizing trips, keeping track of clothing sizes (seriously, there is never just one size that works and kids, omg, they grow crazy fast) homework, activities and trying to find Herobrine in Minecraft, you sort of turn into a robot mom zombie. At least that's the way it feels to me sometimes.

I hope that throughout this book you have found your own "Reiki" experience, some sort of light that clicked on above your head that makes you realize that you too deserve some attention. Perhaps you've tried one of the meditations, howled your intentions at the moon, had a big emotional garage sale, or otherwise discovered how to bring some balance back in your life so you can be (insert your name here) as well as mom, wife, dad, husband, employee, employer, taxi, etc.

Please don't get me wrong here, I'm not a Zen Rockmomstar by any stretch of the imagination. I still get frustrated and turn into a Momster at times (Just ask my kids!). I am human after all, and not one ounce of the spiritual life can take that away.

Parenthood is tough work, the hardest job I've ever had and the one that I cherish most on this earth. Even if you are not a parent, these lessons still can be applied to you in your life. Always find balance, always believe in yourself, always know that you have the power to shape your future and bring your ethereal dreams to a tangible reality.

The spiritual trinity is Breathe, Balance, Live.

Let's all remember to breathe deeply, to bring balance, and to live in the moment whenever possible.

ABOUT THE AUTHOR

I began this writing journey as a young child in Western New York. In my teen years, I won poetry and short story competitions, wrote articles for the school newspaper and received a literary award.

I attended school at Pacific College of Oriental Medicine in Manhattan. Returning home, I began freelance writing, blogging, practicing Reiki, writing and conducting my own guided meditation workshops, and having articles featured in online and print magazines.

My spiritual studies began in my early teens while immersing myself in books at the local bookstores and libraries. I began attending workshops ranging from: pagan religions, spiritualism, crystals, intuition development, meditation, runes, tarot, herbal, aroma, color, and energy therapy to name a few. Basically, any metaphysical/holistic/wellness subject I could devour, I did.

In 2001, I became a Reiki master and began treatments for family and friends. I also conducted intuitive tarot readings throughout this time as well.

I became a mother in 2007 adding another beautiful baby boy in 2009. In 2011, my vision for *Finding Your Spirit: A Mom's Guide to the Universe* became apparent as I realized that I needed a spiritual guidebook to help me balance motherhood with spirituality. Not finding one online or in stores, I decided to write my own.

Now in 2014/2015 I'm ecstatic to have it available to you. I hope you had as much fun reading it and working with the lessons as I had in creating it!

15689340R00089

Made in the USA
Middletown, DE
18 November 2014